THE LAST

ROMAN

Published by The Langley Press, 2024

THE LAST
ROMAN

THE LIFE AND TIMES OF
CASSIODORUS

SIMON WEBB

Also from the Langley Press:

Nicholas Breakspear: The English Pope
The Life and Times of Adelard of Bath
Aaron of Lincoln
What Do We Know About Pontius Pilate?
The Life and Legend of Nicholas Flamel
The Book of Ashoka

For more from the Langley Press, please visit our
website at www.langleypress.co.uk

CONTENTS

Cassiodorus

Prelude

By the end of the fifth century CE, Rome, which had ruled over so many nations, was being fought over by the armies of nations that would have been quite unknown to most Romans in the days of Julius Caesar. To understand the history of this time, it is important to remember that a *nation* and a *country* can be two different things. By the time Theodoric the Ostrogoth had established himself as ruler of Italy in 493 CE, it hardly mattered that his people had started out somewhere in Eastern Europe. They had spread themselves into all sorts of places, and still retained enough of their culture and sense of self to comprise a distinct and coherent group. They were one of the peoples involved in what historians now call the Migration Period, which continued for some three hundred blood-soaked years from around 300 CE.

In those days, there were many nations without countries. A list of modern examples of nations or peoples without a country of their own would include the Kurds, who have significant populations in Turkey, Iran, Iraq, Syria and elsewhere. In Europe, the Basques live in an area that includes parts of both Spain and France, and the Catalans live in part of Spain. Until the foundation of the modern state of Israel in 1948, the Jews were the classic example of a nation without a country, since they had their own distinctive culture and languages, though many of their ancestors had been forced out of the Holy Land by the Romans after 70 CE. It was then that the Temple in Jerusalem was destroyed, leaving only the so-called Wailing Wall that serves as a focus for Jewish worship today. Back in 70 CE, the treasures of the Temple, including a large menorah, were carted off by the troops of the future emperor Titus. The menorah, borne aloft by the Roman troops, can be seen in a relief on the Arch of Titus in Rome. Much of the rest of Jerusalem was also looted and destroyed, and vast numbers of her citizens massacred.

The people of nations without countries have been known to emigrate to escape discrimination and even persecution; like the Jews, such people may long to have their own country. People of such nations who remain where they are may be tempted to hide or play down their distinctive identity, abandon their native culture and 'assimilate'. In the conditions that prevailed at the time of Cassiodorus, hordes of people of various nations, ultimately looking for a place to live, or a different or better place to live, swarmed over Europe and beyond, raiding, burning, pillaging, and sometimes invading and settling. In fact our English word 'horde' comes from the Turkish word *ordu*, originally used the describe a troop of Tartars, nomadic tribesmen from central Asia who are not, however, known to have raided anywhere in Europe until long after Cassiodorus' time.

The history of Britain has been affected by at least three peoples looking for a new homeland, and prepared to carve one out with their swords. According to the English chronicler Bede, a British king called Vortigern invited the Anglo-Saxons into Britain as mercenaries, some forty years before Theodoric became the ruler of Italy. The Anglo-Saxons made allies of the people they were supposed to fight, started to make war against their British masters, and were soon present in such huge numbers across such a large area that a new country was named after them: England. By this time, Britain was no concern of Rome at all: the Romans had pulled out of our islands early in the century in which Cassiodorus was born. Other land-hungry nations who impacted British history were the Vikings and the Normans.

The marauding nations who roamed across Europe, Asia and Africa in the days of Cassiodorus were a threat to almost anyone who had the misfortune to encounter them. More generally, they endangered the stability of the Roman Empire, which then stretched right around the Mediterranean and included the whole of what are now Spain and Portugal, France, Italy, Greece, Turkey, Israel, Egypt and a broad strip along the north coast of Africa.

The Roman response to the threats posed by what we now call the Migration Period was complex: a detailed study of it would fill a much longer book than this one. Of course the Romans *fought* people like the Vandals, a Germanic people who seized large areas of North Africa, and several Mediterranean islands; but they also sought to play such groups off against each other, divide and rule, turn them into allies, recruit large numbers of them into the Roman armies, and pay others to fight as mercenaries (as the Britons had tried to do with the Anglo-Saxons).

Suffice it to say that by the time Cassiodorus was born, people whom many Romans would have regarded as barbarians from the wild lands of northern Europe held positions of great power both inside and outside the Roman Empire. It was one such powerful foreigner, a Goth called Odoacer, who deposed the last emperor of Rome in 476, some ten years before Cassiodorus was born. The unfortunate emperor's name was Romulus Augustulus, whose names, ironically, included those of the founder, and first emperor, of Rome.

A teenager when he became emperor, in 2006 Augustulus was the subject of a biography by Adrian Murdoch, the title of which also includes the phrase 'the last Roman'. Many other books have been written about 'the last Roman' or 'the last of the Romans', some of them fiction. The deposed emperor Augustulus probably outlived his deposer Odoacer, who was murdered in 493. The last emperor of the western empire may have died in 511 or even later, as the Goth conqueror had spared his life and allowed him to live safely in a castle in the Campania region of Italy. It is said that Odoacer did not have the teenage emperor done away with partly because of his youth, but also because of his good looks.

If some ancestor of Odoacer had deposed a much earlier Roman emperor such as, for instance, Tiberius (who ruled in the first century CE), history would have been turned inside-out and upside-down, and the Romans might have vanished from its pages altogether. In the event, Odoacer's coup was not as momentous as it might seem, even though the Goth usurper insisted that there would now no longer be any more emperors in Rome, since he himself refused to assume the title. Like his successor Theodoric, Odoacer still paid lip-service and more to the remaining Roman emperor in the East. This has something to do with a trait of people living during these times, which was excessive respect for the past.

If something (like an empire) or somebody (like an aristocrat) was felt to have connections to the deep past, they or it tended to be revered. This is partly why the Romans kept celebrating pagan festivals and admiring statues of the old gods many years after most of them had become Christians; why they also sought to preserve useless, empty, obsolete old buildings, and why, for instance, they continued to respect the Roman senate and its institutions long after they had any real power or significance. This respect for old things was surely part of the motivation that led both Cassiodorus and his contemporary Boethius to revere ancient Greek and Latin texts that were written long before the emergence of Christianity.

Another effect of this ancient sense that even more ancient times had been better evidently caused many Italians living under Gothic monarchs in Cassiodorus' time to long for the return of Roman rulers and full re-incorporation back into the old empire.

Something old, like the empire itself, that was widely revered, was the city of Rome, though by the year 476 she had not been the capital of the empire she gave her name for nearly a century and a half, since the emperor Constantine had made his city of Constantinople (now Istanbul in

Turkey) the capital in 330 CE. Over forty years before that, the empire, which by that time had become too large to be governed in one piece, was split into two halves, the western and eastern empires. The eastern empire, ruled from Constantinople, comprised Greece and everything to the east of Greece, while the western empire, ruled from Rome, covered everything to the west, including Italy itself, France, Spain and, at that time, Great Britain south of Hadrian's Wall.

As if Rome had not lost enough status to Constantinople, which now commanded the richer and more sophisticated half of the empire, early in the fifth century the status of capital of the western empire was transferred from Rome to Ravenna, on Italy's north-east coast. From there Odoacer ruled his new kingdom, wisely preserving the old administrative structures, including an impressive imperial council, one of whose members may have been the father of the ill-fated philosopher Boethius, of whom more later.

As the years rolled by, the status of Rome as a centre for secular power was diminished as the prestige of the bishops of Rome, the popes, said to be successors of St Peter, the fisherman and disciple of Jesus, grew and grew. Under Odoacer's successor, Rome was not even the second capital. When he believed Ravenna to be unsafe, Theodoric decamped to Verona in the far north-east.

In fact Rome seems to have meant so little to Cassiodorus' master Theodoric that he may only ever have spent six month in the city, in 500 CE. This was a triumphal visit, with ecstatic greetings from the Roman citizens (by then rather thin on the ground) and chariot-races held in the king's honour. Before he left the city on the Tiber, his majesty promised to fund re-building in the city, and to distribute the equivalent of over seven hundred metric tons of free corn to the citizens every year.

Ravenna's exalted status at this time is the reason why it is such a treasure-house of Byzantine-period culture, where visitors can admire the strange architecture of the time, and the stunning mosaics. Part of the city is now a UNESCO World Heritage Site: buildings Cassiodorus would have known include the sixth-century Basilica of San Vitale, and the earlier Mausoleum of Galla Placida. In both, visitors can marvel at astonishing mosaics. In one of his celebrated letters, Cassiodorus revealed a weakness for this amazingly durable art-form. Speaking as his master Theodoric ordering more mosaics for Ravenna from one Agepitus, he wrote:

From Art proceeds this gift, which conquers Nature. And thus the discoloured surface of the marble is woven into the loveliest variety of pictures; the value of the work, now as always, being increased by the minute labour which has to be expended on the production of the Beautiful.

(trans. Hodgkin)

In his biography of Theodoric, Thomas Hodgkin reminds us that when we look at one of these mosaics, many of which incorporate gold-covered tiles, we are looking at something very close to the colours early medieval worshippers would have seen. This is not the case with old paintings or frescoes. In a metaphor worthy of Cassiodorus himself, Hodgkin calls the city of Ravenna 'a boulder-stone left by the ice-drift of the dissolving Empire'. Gazing on some mosaics Cassiodorus himself might have seen, Hodgkin reflects that they were made at a time when 'there were still men living on the earth who worshipped the Olympian Jupiter, and that the name of Mohammed, son of Abdallah, was unknown in the world'.

Though Odoacer was not an emperor, and in fact had sent the imperial crown jewels to Constantinople, he began to be seen as a threat by the eastern emperor, then a man called Zeno the Isaurian. Zeno also feared Theodoric the Ostrogoth, and seems to have decided to play off these two formidable threats against each other. Zeno made Theodoric a consul and a patrician of the Roman empire, both great honours, and persuaded him to invade Italy. After doing badly in a series of battles, Odoacer retreated to his capital of Ravenna and managed to fend off Theodoric's army for three years.

At last, in March 493, the opponents made a treaty, which Theodoric broke by personally stabbing Odoacer to death, and massacring all his followers. Theodoric now found himself the master of the Ostrogothic kingdom, which at its greatest extent included not only Italy and Sicily, but a large area stretching north and east from the north-eastern shores of the Adriatic, including what are now the countries of Slovenia, Croatia, and Bosnia and Herzogovina.

The fall of Odoacer happened when Cassiodorus, the hero of this book, was perhaps eight years old; but despite centuries of scholarship, the exact years of Cassiodorus' birth and death have never been determined. Theodoric was thirty-nine or forty when he became king of Italy. Like Odoacer,

Italy's new master opted to maintain the administrative structures that had been used to govern the empire for centuries. These included a hierarchy comprising a bewildering number of ranks and offices, with Latin titles that resemble some English words still in use today. These included the *Nobilissimi*, the *Illustres*, the *Spectabiles*, the *Perfectissimi* and the *Egregii*.

Whereas his predecessor Odoacer had only ruled for thirteen years, Theodoric ruled for thirty-three, before he died of dysentery in 526, when Cassiodorus would have been around forty years old. This means that Cassiodorus, very much a Roman, grew up and reached middle age while Italy was under the control of Odoacer and Theodoric, neither of whom were Romans or even Italians in terms of their ancestry – men whose culture and native language were quite different from those of Cassiodorus and his people.

The subject of this biography came from an ancient, aristocratic Roman family, and his father, also called Cassiodorus, was serving Theodoric in the lofty position of praetorian prefect by the time Cassiodorus turned twenty. This was originally a military position, to do with the praetorian guards who protected the emperor and his capital, but by Theodoric's time the praetorian prefect was something like a prime minister. Like a British monarch today, Theodoric remained head of state, while his praetorian prefect did much of the practical work of ruling. The difference was that whereas our modern British kings and queens have little or no actual power, the Gothic kings of Italy could really do anything they liked, and as a consequence got up to some very shocking stuff.

It was around this time that, under the auspices of his powerful father, Cassiodorus became a *consiliarus*, in this case a sort of legal assistant to his dad. It was while he was in this position that Cassiodorus had the opportunity to deliver a panegyric, a speech in praise of Theodoric, who by this time had ruled Italy for some seven years. The king of both the Italians and the Ostrogoths heard the young man's speech and found it so convincing that he immediately promoted the speaker through the highest ranks of his government, making him one of the half-dozen most powerful men in Italy.

His official title was at first that of *quaestor*, the chief orator or spokesman for the Roman government. As such, Cassiodorus was not only required to speak for Theodoric, but also to deal with much of his correspondence, and write out key edicts in fitting language. In his biography of Theodoric, Hodgkin suggests that Cassiodorus was well-suited to this job as he 'was never so happy as when he was wrapping up some commonplace thought in a garment of sonorous but turgid rhetoric'. He remained the go-to guy for any tricky piece of writing that needed doing: even when he was promoted out of the ranks of the quaestors, to the higher position of master of the offices, the quaestors turned to him 'when pure eloquence was needed'.

A sense that nobody did it better than Cassiodorus seems to have been part of the author's motivation for putting together a selection of his letters. Since something like all these letters had evidently been 'passed' by Theodoric or his officials, they could serve as models for future writers. The author even includes 'model' or 'template' letters that can be copied out and adapted.

Tomb of Theodoric

The King and Cassiodorus

We know about Cassiodorus' time as a very superior servant or minister of Theodoric and his Gothic successors because of his most famous work, those collected letters, called *Variae* by their author, because he felt that they were extremely varied. They were certainly written on a wide variety of subjects and addressed to a selection of different sorts of people holding various ranks within the hierarchy of Rome and Rome's heirs.

The letters are also written in different styles – Cassiodorus calls these the 'humble', 'middle' and 'supreme' styles. The humble style 'seems to creep along the ground in the very expression of its thought'; the middle style 'is neither swollen with self-importance nor shrunk into littleness', while the supreme style 'is raised to the very highest pitch of oratory'. It is necessary, the author asserts, to write in different styles if one is writing to different sorts of people – kings, officers of the court and sometimes 'the very humblest of the people'. There are, moreover, people who are 'jaded with much reading', others 'who skim lightly over the surface, tasting here and there', and a third group 'who are devoid of a taste for letters'.

Cassiodorus claims, modestly, that he cannot hope to pretend to true mastery of the supreme style with its 'exquisite phraseology'. Generations of readers have fervently wished that he had never attempted this elevated style, which sometimes renders his writings over-elaborate and hard to follow. In the introduction to his translated selections from the *Variae*, Hodgkin asserts that throughout the letters 'the style is undoubtedly a bad one', and goes on to complain about 'sentence after sentence of verbose and flaccid Latin', where the 'central thought' comes over as 'the merest and most obvious commonplace, a piece of tinsel wrapped in endless folds of tissue paper'.

James O'Donnell, author of an indispensable 1979 biography of Cassiodorus, defends aspects of his style. Certainly the Roman goes off on tangents that can sometimes be as fascinating as the digressions of Laurence Sterne, eighteenth-century author of the unique *Life and Opinions of Tristram Shandy*. A letter to one Honorius, prefect of Rome, laments that some brass elephants that adorned the city's Via Sacra are ageing badly, then goes on to favour the prefect with a lot of information about real-life elephants that can have been of absolutely no practical use to him in his task of restoring brass ones.

The elephant, Cassiodorus reminds Honorius, can live to be more than a thousand years old. She is the most intelligent of all animals, since she worships God and, though she will bow to a good human ruler, she will not honour a tyrant in this way. She has a remarkably long memory, and her breath can cure headaches. This is a fairly typical digression of Cassiodorus'; and it confirms O'Donnell's observation that animals and natural history in general were never far from the author's mind.

As the writer of these letters, Cassiodorus was often acting as the mouthpiece for whatever ruler had required him to write them. Theodoric in particular needed someone to deal with his correspondence, as despite years spent as a princely hostage in the cultured atmosphere of Constantinople, he seems to have been barely literate, and had to sign his name using a kind of golden stencil (it is said that the eastern emperor Justin had to do the same thing).

Early in the *Variae*, the letter-writer finds himself having to praise his own family, on the occasion of his father's promotion to the status of patrician, during the time of Theodoric. The letter was directed to the Roman senate, a body of men Cassiodorus treated to an account of his father's virtues, and the solid worth of the men of his family as demonstrated through three generations. The *Cassiodori* earned the best kind of fame, were fine orators and formidable warriors, enjoyed good health and were all, it seems, very tall. If our Cassiodorus followed the family tradition of loftiness, this may have helped him relate to the various Gothic kings and queens for whom he worked, since on average the northerners tended to be taller than their Italian subjects. He could literally communicate with them on their own level.

A portrait of Cassiodorus that appears in a twelfth-century German manuscript now kept at the university library of Leiden shows what could be intended for a tall man, in this case one with a long, thin, plaited brown beard and thick, curly hair. This version of our author sits on a kind of throne, holding a large book open on his knees, with one long, slender index finger held up in an attitude of teaching. The Leiden manuscript contains a version of Cassiodorus' *Variae* and a Life of Cassiodorus' master Theodoric the Great, bound together with the *Didascalion*, a kind of encyclopaedia, written by Hugo of Saint-Victor, a twelfth century French theologian. The manuscript (Leiden ms. Vul. 46) also includes some treatises on the Old Testament, by the author of the *Didascalion*.

Because our Cassiodorus and his father had the same name, there has been a tendency for historians to mix them up. This could not happen so easily in our Cassiodorus' lifetime, when he was usually called 'Senator', an odd name that he had been given as a child, long before he could ever have been appointed to Rome's august parliament.

Cassiodorus' grandfather, also called Cassiodorus, had served as *tribunus et notarius* under the emperor Valentinian III. A tribune was like a modern army colonel, and a *notarius* was someone who was trusted to draw up official documents, as our Cassiodorus was. Although Valentian III was assassinated some thirty years before our Cassiodorus was born, his reign was plagued by just the kinds of warlike, mobile nations from the north and east that had produced the Goth Odoacer and the Ostrogoth Theodoric, both of whom made themselves kings of Italy. In the time of Valentinian, and of Cassiodorus' grandfather, the biggest threat was from the Huns, led by the notorious Attila.

21

Cassiodorus' grandfather was a friend of the most illustrious Roman military commander of the time, Flavius Aetius. Such were Aetius's fine qualities that he has also sometimes been called 'the last Roman' or 'the last of the Romans'. In the way of great generals throughout much of Roman history, Aetius attracted the jealousy and suspicion of the emperor, and was personally killed by his imperial majesty and an accomplice, in 454. Cassiodorus' grandfather accompanied Carpilio, a son of Aetius, on an embassy to Attila, and, according to his grandson's account in the *Variae*:

He looked undaunted on the man before whom the Empire quailed. Calm in conscious strength, he despised all those terrible wrathful faces that scowled around him. He did not hesitate to meet the full force of the invectives of the madman who fancied himself about to grasp the Empire of the world. He found the King insolent; he left him pacified; and so ably did he argue down all his slanderous pretexts for dispute that though the Hun's interest was to quarrel with the richest Empire in the world, he nevertheless condescended to seek its favour.

Grandfather's encounter with the Hunnish chief allowed him to 'bring back the peace which men had despaired of'. After playing his part in this diplomatic triumph, the grandfather was offered rich rewards, but preferred to retire to the family's lands at Brutii in what is now Calabria, on the toe of Italy. His own father, our Cassiodorus' great-grandfather, who was also called Cassiodorus, had helped to defend both this region and nearby Sicily from the Vandals, who as we know occupied a strip of North Africa and several

Mediterranean islands to the west of Italy, in the days of Theodoric.

Evidently, their lands in Calabria exerted a strong attraction on the *Cassiodori*, wherever they found themselves. Our Cassiodorus waxes lyrical about the region in a letter written for his young master Athalaric to one Severus, a recipient of several letters from this source. In the letter, Cassiodorus' habit of going off at a tangent causes him to contradict himself and almost blunt the point of the letter altogether. The point was that Athalaric wanted Severus to talk to some of the local bigwigs down in Calabria – 'the *possessores* and *curiales* of Bruttii' – to try to persuade them to spend less time on their farms, and instead live for at least some of the time in the region's cities, for 'we are sure that you will agree with us that cities are the chief ornament of human society':

Let the wild beasts live in fields and woods: men ought to draw together into cities. Even among birds we see that those of gentle disposition – like thrushes, storks, and doves – love to flock together, while the greedy hawk, intent on its bloody pastime, seeks solitude.

Here again we see Cassiodorus' tendency to turn to the animal kingdom for examples of how people should or should not live. Unfortunately the letter-writer undermines his argument against country life by admitting that, at least in the case of Calabria:

In truth it is a lovely land. Ceres and Pallas have crowned it with their respective gifts (corn and oil); the plains are green with pastures, the slopes are purple with vineyards. Above all is it rich in its vast herds of horses, and no wonder, since the dense shade of its forests protects them from the bites of flies, and provides them with ever-verdant pasture even in the height of summer. Cool waters flow from its lofty heights; fair harbours on both its shores woo the commerce of the world.

Among the virtues of his own father that Cassiodorus opted to point out, in his letter to the senate composed for Theodoric, the author mentioned his wealth, which meant that he owned so many fine horses that they exceeded in number those of Theodoric himself. No doubt some of the lucky horses mentioned in Athalaric's letter to Severus, that could shelter in the forest and avoid insect-bites, were descendants of those owned by Cassiodorus' dad. To short-circuit the king's envy, the old man made presents of some of his beasts to the Ostrogoth, thus supplying horses to the Goth's army. Cassiodorus' letter to the senate also mentions 'a cousin of the *Cassiodori*' called Heliodorus, who was a much-admired and long-serving prefect of the eastern empire. 'Thus the family,' Cassiodorus remarks in a typical rhetorical flight, 'conspicuous both in the eastern and western world, has two eyes with which it shines with equal brilliancy in each senate'.

The presence of Heliodorus in Constantinople (which is attested from independent sources) and the name 'Cassiodorus' itself suggest that the author's family may have originated in Syria, since a god called Zeus Cassius was worshipped at Antioch in pagan times and later. As ancient Syrians, Cassiodorus' ancestors would probably have spoken Greek, which may be connected to the fact that their family estates in Calabria were once part of a Greek colony down there. Perhaps part of the family had drifted west, leaving some members still in the east, and those became the ancestors of Heliodorus. If we accept the idea that the name 'Cassiodorus' had something to do with Zeus Cassius, then both the *Cassiodori* and their cousin Heliodorus, who were supposed to be Christians, were named for pagan gods, since Helios was a sun-god.

Since he came from such an illustrious and well-established family, and since he insisted on showing a great deal of learning in his writings, we can be certain that Cassiodorus was pretty well-read by the time he caught Theodoric's eye and ear, though at the time he may only have been in his early twenties. Like most young men of his class, his studies would have centred on philosophy and rhetoric, the name for the second of which is now a pejorative term, which means that the role of rhetoric in Roman education, and life in general, is often misunderstood.

When we dismiss a speech as 'rhetoric' today we usually mean that it seems artificial and insincere; put together for effect, but with no real underpinning in fact or emotion. For the Romans and the medieval inheritors of their classical culture rhetoric covered the whole wide business of expression and communication. In a world where writing was the pre-eminent form of communication, with public speeches coming a remote second in terms of importance, the choice of words, of style and approach, were crucial.

In our multi-media world, the use of words seems less important, though misuse of the wrong words can get people in the public eye into very serious trouble. Since anyone connected to electronic media can both see and hear powerful people and their representatives who have to (or choose to) exhibit themselves in this way, a good voice and a photogenic look have become all-important. These were surely key to the popularity of US president Ronald Reagan, once a Hollywood screen actor, who was certainly no wordsmith or spinner of phrases.

By the time Cassiodorus was old enough to read advanced texts, there was plenty of literature available to him that could inform his own development as a communicator. This would have included the recorded speeches of the Roman politician Cicero (106-43 BCE), and of the earlier Cato the Elder, whose speeches now only survive as fragments. Cassiodorus would also have known the works of Virgil and Ovid, 'Augustan' poets who lived at the time of the emperor Augustus (died 14 CE).

The works of various Greek authors would also have been known to Cassiodorus, but he may have known little Greek himself. He also knew and worked with his close contemporary Anicius Manlius Severinus Boethius, known as Boethius, who is remembered as one of the greatest writers of the age, and was related to Cassiodorus.

In the same way that figures like Aetius and Cassiodorus are sometimes named as the last Romans, Boethius's *On the Consolations of Philosophy* is regarded by some as the last great masterpiece written in something like classical Latin, and its author is sometimes called the last of the Roman philosophers. Boethius's distinguished father-in-law Quintus Aurelius Memmius Symmachus was also a well-regarded author whom Cassiodorus would have known, but hardly anything from his work survives.

We know that Cassiodorus was related to both Boethius and Symmachus because of a document called the *Anecdoton holderi*, part of which seems to consist of fragments of a letter in which Cassiodorus boasted about the literary achievements of members of his family. As well as confirming the family link, the *Anecdoton holderi*, which was unknown until late in the nineteenth century, also provides evidence that Boethius really did write certain texts that were previously attributed to him with some hesitation.

It is hard to imagine how a well-educated and aristocratic young Roman like Cassiodorus would have been able to communicate with an illiterate foreign warlord like Theodoric. There was even an age-difference of some thirty years, which put the Ostrogoth into the generation of his *quaestor*'s parents. But communicate they did, and after his master's death in 526 Cassiodorus wrote about the '*gloriosa colloquia*' that they had shared. In the relevant letter from the *Variae*, this time written for Theodoric's successor, his grandson Athalaric, the author rose to the odd task of praising and recommending himself, on the occasion of his own promotion to the lofty position of praetorian prefect, which his father had held years before.

Writing as Athalaric, who was only a child when his grandfather died, Cassiodorus points to his friendly relations with the boy's grandfather as one of the factors that make him suitable for such a lofty position. 'Athalaric' writes that Theodoric, who was anxious by nature, was able to lay aside his cares, 'while you [Cassiodorus] supported the weight of the royal counsels with the strength of your eloquence'. This would seem to suggest that when a thorny question of the government of Italy was worrying Theodoric, reassuring speeches from Cassiodorus could help him relax. But even when the king of Italy was enjoying some down-time, he found the company of his bright young friend diverting:

> . . . he would ask you to tell him the stories in which wise men of old have clothed their maxims, that by his own deeds he might equal the ancient heroes. The courses of the stars, the ebb and flow of the sea, the marvels of springing fountains, into all these subjects would that most acute questioner inquire, so that by his diligent investigations into the nature of things, he seemed to be a philosopher in the purple.

It seems that Cassiodorus was giving Theodoric a sort of crash-course in Roman ethics, literature and science, among other things, though he evidently did not require his student to read anything for himself, or write any assignments as homework. Hodgkin who, like Edward Gibbon, regarded Theodoric as a genuine hero, suggests in his biography of the Ostrogoth that his majesty may also have brought some worthwhile content of his own to the table:

> . . . the young, learned, and eloquent Roman poured forth for his master the stored up wine of generations of philosophers and poets, while the kingly barbarian doubtless unfolded some of the propositions of that more difficult science, the knowledge of men, which he had acquired by long and arduous years of study in the council-chamber, on the mountain-march, and on the battle-field.

Some of the scientific content of these *gloriosa colloquia*, which seems to have piqued the king's curiosity, may have been drawn from the *De Rerum Natura* ('Of the Nature of Things') by the Roman philosopher Lucretius, who died around 55 BCE. This was a poem which, among other things, set out Roman ideas about what we would now call astronomy.

Cassiodorus' account of his relationship with Theodoric, as conveyed in his letter written to and about himself, but as if it had been penned by Athalaric, can be put together with the letters he wrote for Athalaric's grandfather to create a fairly detailed but hazy picture of what Cassiodorus actually did for Theodoric during his years in public office. His contributions fall into two categories, divided by a very fuzzy line. His official duties; drafting speeches, letters and other documents, could presumably have been done with little or no personal contact with the Ostrogoth king. His duties as Theodoric's personal counsellor and educator seem to have required prolonged personal contact.

In his letter about himself, Cassiodorus insists that Theodoric valued him as a friend not just because of his learning but also because he was honest and ethical. There was no taint in the man, we are told, of the graft and corruption we would tend to associate with a declining, divided empire. Although Hodgkin, usually ready to defend both Cassiodorus and his royal master, suggests that the former was indeed something of a paragon, it is still possible to view the relationship between the two men in a harsher light. Was Cassiodorus able to conceal nefarious goings-on with his bright, youthful manner? Can it be that he had no real affection for Theodoric, and was merely flattering him? Were those eloquent speeches that seemed to lighten the king's load of anxiety merely designed to hoodwink him and lull him into a false sense of security? He was calming the troubled king as David did Saul with the sweet tones of his harp: but then David did become Saul's enemy. (As we will see, in one of his letters Cassiodorus mentioned how David drove out Saul's evil spirits.)

We can deduce from the *Variae* that Cassiodorus was not the only Roman who was able to befriend the king in this way. One Artemidorus was also able to do it, and like Cassiodorus he rose to giddy heights in Theodoric's administration. In one of the *Variae*, 'Theodoric' writes that Artemidorus, like Cassiodorus a scion of a noble old family, pleased his majesty, who 'was often refreshed after the cares of State by an hour of his charming converse'. As we will see, a man called Cyprian served the same function, but his speciality was to do it during horseback rides with Theodoric.

Both Hodgkin and Gibbon suggest that Theodoric and Cassiodorus were united in a mission to assert the best of the new Gothic spirit, to preserve the honest old Roman ways of doing things, and to restore order and the comforts of *civilitas* to Italy. In his *Decline and Fall of the Roman Empire*, Gibbon is particularly harsh about Cassiodorus' baroque writing style, implying that an author who wrote like that could not be trusted, and asserts that:

The reputation of Theodoric may repose with more confidence on the visible peace and prosperity of a reign of thirty-three years; the unanimous esteem of his own times, and the memory of his wisdom and courage, his justice and humanity, which was deeply impressed on the minds of the Goths and Italians.

Gibbon's catalogue of Theodoric's virtues is reminiscent of a short book on the subject of the human soul that Cassiodorus wrote some time after his old master died. In his *De anima*, the author mentioned a sense of justice, and also prudence, fortitude, temperance, contemplation, judgement and memory as virtuous characteristics of the soul that good people might be in contact with.

The benefits of the reign of Theodoric the paragon were tangible, and in some cases quite literally concrete. Repeatedly in Cassiodorus' *Variae*, we come across letters sent by Theodoric to local officials, encouraging them to build, re-build and restore, but also to preserve, venerable old buildings, the materials from which might otherwise be stolen for illicit re-use. In a letter to one Sabinianus, a *vir spectabilis*, Cassiodorus, writing as Theodoric, reminds his correspondent that:

It is important to preserve as well as to create. We are earnestly anxious to keep the walls of Rome in good repair, and have therefore ordered the Lucrine port to furnish 25,000 tiles annually for this purpose. See that this is done, that the cavities which have been formed by the fall of stones may be roofed over with tiles, and so preserved, and that thus we may deserve the thanks of ancient kings, to whose works we have given immortal youth.

Under Theodoric Verona, the northern city that would later become famous as the home of the star-crossed lovers

Romeo and Juliet, was fortified with newly-constructed city walls, its thirst quenched by a refurbished aqueduct. At Pavia (then called Ticinum) Theodoric built new defensive walls, a palace, baths and an amphitheatre, and in his capital Ravenna, the new king restored Trajan's aqueduct and completed the construction of a royal palace. The citizens of Ravenna had reason to be particularly grateful for the restoration of their aqueduct. Set in marshy country, their city had long struggled to find good drinking-water, and it was said that at times wine could be bought cheaper.

The one surviving wall of a building long identified as part of Theodoric's palace in Ravenna is now thought not to have been part of his palace at all. Excavations carried out in the early years of the last century revealed the remains of the Ostrogoth's real palace, identified thanks to the name of Theodoric that could still be seen on the lead sewage pipes that had served the building. This palace, where perhaps Cassiodorus and the king had enjoyed their *gloriosa colloquia,* seems to have been surprisingly modest.

Nearby is the cathedral Theodoric built for himself and his fellow-Arians, followers of the Arian version of Christianity that was popular among the Goths, but regarded as heretical by the Pope in Rome and the emperors in Constantinople. On the south wall of this church, which is now called San Apollinare Nuovo, is a mosaic showing Theodoric's palace as it must have looked when the mosaicists were working there. The building in the mosaic has the word 'PALATIO' inscribed above its grand entrance, but after the church ceased to be an Arian place of worship what were probably mosaics showing Theodoric and members of his family were obliterated. The work was badly done, as one can still see some of the hands of the lost figures.

The loss of what might have been a mosaic of Theodoric mounted on a horse is keenly felt by historians, as its survival would have allowed them to get some idea of how the great man actually looked. No images of him survive, and later painters and sculptors have had to use their imaginations, sometimes giving the Ostrogoth a ludicrous winged helmet and elaborate whiskers. There is a similar lack of reliable images of Cassiodorus.

As well as making his subjects feel safe within the new walls that defended their cities, Theodoric tried to secure peace by marrying his daughters off into the families of other barbarian rulers. Agriculture revived and flourished under his leadership, and Italy began to export grain, whereas for centuries the Romans had had to import it, from Egypt for instance, which was once considered the bread-basket of the empire.

If Cassiodorus was using his particular skills, and the venerable reputation of his family, to smooth the path of the peace, prosperity, wisdom, courage, justice and humanity that Italy's new king was working so hard to promote, it is hard to find fault with that. But not all of the author's Roman contemporaries were happy that the source of all these benefits was a foreign invader.

ANICIUS MANLIUS SEVERINUS BOETIUS.

Ex votus Statua marmorea
quæ est Romæ.

H. Bary
sculp

Boethius

The picture of Cassiodorus and Theodoric engaged in their *gloriosa colloquia,* in the modest royal palace at Ravenna, while Italy enjoyed a few years of peace and prosperity, is an attractive one, but the fate of one of the former's close contemporaries, who was in many respects similar to the subject of this biography, reveals the savage side of both Theodoric and his times. The ill-fated one was the aforementioned Boethius, who may have been born around the same time as Cassiodorus, enjoyed a similar career in the service of Theodoric, but was not lucky enough to be so long-lived.

Born into the noble and ancient Roman family of the *Anicii,* Boethius lost his father very young, and was raised by his future father-in-law, Symmachus. It seems that the orphan was something of an infant prodigy, whose educational attainment was even more distinguished than that of Cassiodorus himself. Boethius, who may have been educated in Greece or elsewhere in the Greek-speaking East, had a superb grasp of the Greek language, knowledge of which was becoming rare, by his time, in the West. He later became an important translator of classic Greek works into Latin.

The precocious young man somehow came to the attention of Theodoric. One consequence of this was that Cassiodorus was detailed to write to Boethius in the person of King Theodoric, to convey Theodoric's orders. Some of these letters are preserved in the *Variae*. In one of them, the king asks Boethius, who was by this time a patrician and an *illustris*, to look into a possible case of fraud. It seems that an official called the *arcarius praefectorum* had attempted to pay members of the praetorian guard with coins that were not of the full weight.

In another letter, Boethius is asked to obtain or perhaps construct a water-clock and a sundial as a gift from Theodoric to the king of the Burgundians. Of course the long-winded Cassiodorus could not put the request into a short letter. He had to remind Boethius of the value of gifts to 'royal neighbours' as what we would now call 'soft power': 'often what arms cannot obtain the offices of kindness bring to pass . . . it will be a great gain to us [meaning Theodoric, using the royal 'we'] that the Burgundians should daily look upon something sent by us which will appear to them little short of miraculous'.

Evidently, Theodoric via Cassiodorus was asking Boethius for a more elaborate water-clock than the most basic type, known to the ancient Egyptians, which was simply a bowl out of which water could flow at a steady rate, with marks on the inside of the bowl corresponding to hours passed. Such a model had to be more complex than it might seem from the description above because the ancient Egyptians had longer hours in the summer than they did in the winter, when the days are shorter. Some of the more sophisticated types that were known to the ancients could be adjusted to allow for this seasonal difference in the lengths of the hours.

Since the king was asking for something that would appear 'miraculous' it is likely that he would only have been satisfied with a *clepsydra* (as the Greeks called them) that could do rather more than just tell the time at any time of year. The Greeks had developed clocks that rang bells, blew trumpets and opened and closed doors to show little figures of people.

It seems odd that the Burgundian king should have wanted both a water-clock *and* a sun-dial, but it may be that by using both of these together he would be able tell time during the night with the water-clock, and during the day with the sun-dial. The sun-dial could also be used to check the accuracy of the water-clock if both were run simultaneously on a sunny day. Like most clockwork timepieces, the water-clock could then be adjusted to improve its accuracy.

In his letter, Cassiodorus tells Boethius that he is the best man for the job of supplying these devices, since he is steeped in Greek philosophy, and had translated many works, including scientific and mathematical ones, from Greek into Latin. In the letter Cassiodorus wrote to accompany Theodoric's gifts to the Burgundian king, he wrote:

Let [Burgundy] arrange her daily actions by the movements of God's great lights; let her nicely adjust the moments of each hour. In mere confusion passes the order of life when this accurate division of time is unknown. Men are like the beasts, if they only know the passage of the hours by the pangs of hunger, and have no greater certainty as to the flight of time than such as is afforded them by their bellies. For certainty is undoubtedly meant to be entwined in human actions.

Some people are so disciplined in their writing habits that they would find it impossible to inflate a simple request to make or get hold of two gadgets into such a lengthy communication. What seems to have happened repeatedly in Cassiodorus' case is that thoughts of something like a water-clock or a sundial set off all sorts of associations in his head that he simply had to set down.

In his letter to Boethius about the gifts to the Burgundian king, Cassiodorus' mind wandered to mechanical devices in general, and he mentioned 'a machine' that had 'been made to exhibit the courses of the planets and the causes of eclipses'. This may have been a simple orrery, a mechanical device designed to demonstrate how what we now call the solar system worked. In Cassiodorus' day such a device would have had the earth at the centre, with the planets, moon, sun and stars rotating around it.

It is possible, however, that what the author had in mind was rather more than a sort of educational toy, and something like the celebrated Antikythera mechanism, recovered from the bottom of the Mediterranean in 1901. Modern techniques have allowed researchers to get a fuller picture of what the Antikythera was capable of doing: it seems that it could be used to predict eclipses of the sun and other astronomical phenomena, which the ancient Greeks who made the device took very seriously, as they thought they could influence events down on earth. It is strange to think that when Cassiodorus sat down to write to Boethius, the Antikythera mechanism had probably already been on the sea-bed for hundreds of years.

We should not forget that whether Cassiodorus was thinking of something like the Antikythera mechanism when he wrote to Boethius, he was officially writing in the person of King Theodoric. It may be that his majesty thought of two time-pieces as gifts for the king of the Burgundians because he himself had learned about various scientific matters such as the mechanical contrivances of the Greeks, during his conversations with Cassiodorus.

One advantage for Theodoric of leaving one of the more complicated water-clocks with the Burgundian king may have been that, since expertise in such matters may have been lacking at the court of the receiver of the present, Theodoric may have had to leave an expert or two behind to help out with the device. These technicians could have acted as spies for the Gothic king of Italy.

Later in the *Variae*, we learn that, through Cassiodorus, Theodoric asked Boethius to obtain another present for a rival king, the king of the Franks. This time the gift was a human being: a harper. Again, Cassiodorus could not keep the request simple. As well as complimenting Boethius on his own musical taste and knowledge, he treated his correspondent to a précis of his own musical knowledge, and reflections on the musicians' art. Cassiodorus also explored the links between music, oratory and poetry, and mentioned

David's ability to drive devils out of Saul using music. 'We have indulged ourselves in a pleasant digression,' Cassiodorus concludes:

> . . . because it is always agreeable to talk of learning with the learned; but be sure to get us that *Citharoedus* [player of the *cithara* – a sort of lyre], who will go forth like another Orpheus to charm the beast-like hearts of the Barbarians. You will thus both obey us and render yourself famous.

However much commentators on Cassiodorus may complain about his long-winded style, there was surely some logic to his decision to couch these requests made to Boethius in extended pieces of prose. A very short request, imposing such tricky and time-consuming tasks, might have seemed brisk and dismissive. As it was, Cassiodorus flattered his correspondent with the length and complexity of his letters.

The tasks Theodorus gave to Boethius via Cassiodorus, which are recorded in the *Variae*, confer honour on the recipient of the letters, but these were by no means the only honours Boethius received during his life. In 510, when he may only have been thirty years old, Boethius became a consul. To understand what this meant in sixth-century Ravenna we must remember again the reverence the people cherished for the past. When Rome had been a republic it had been ruled by two consuls working under the powerful censor. The consuls changed each year. When Rome acquired an emperor the consuls became less relevant or powerful, but the office was still honoured, and Cassiodorus himself became a consul in 514. He also wrote a short history of the world, his *Chronica*, most of which consists of a long list of consuls with occasional breaks in the list in which events such as the birth of Jesus Christ are inserted.

Though most consuls had to share the office with an equal, Boethius had been a consul alone: in 522, his sons became joint consuls which, together with the other posts they held, had held or would hold in the hierarchy, was a great honour for himself and his family.

It seems incredible that only two or three years after his sons had been joint consuls Boethius should have been tortured and beaten to death, on the orders of Theodoric, in a prison in the Italian city of Pavia. What had happened? It seems that as Theodoric approached the age of seventy the open-minded monarch who had enjoyed all those *gloriosa colloquia* with the enlightened Cassiodorus was beginning to become paranoid and vengeful. Relations with the eastern empire were strained, and there were religious tensions between the Arians and the adherents of the alternative version of Christianity offered by the pope in Rome. A couple of years after Boethius was killed, Pope John I died in prison, where Theodoric had put him on a charge of conspiracy.

The Ostrogoth king suspected that some of his most powerful Roman subjects, who were also Roman-style or orthodox Christians, might be plotting against him with the eastern emperor, then the Justin of whom it was said that, like Theodoric, he was obliged to sign his name using a stencil. While there was certainly a pro-eastern party in the West, there were also thoroughly Roman allies of the Ostrogoth monarchy who sided with Theodoric. One of these

41

was a man called Cyprian, who claimed to have discovered a conspiracy against Theodoric during a visit to Constantinople. The details are hazy, but Boethius was implicated, and began his doomed stint in prison.

Incarcerated at Pavia, Boethius, who had already distinguished himself as a writer, wrote one of the enduring classics of Western literature. His *Consolation of Philosophy* was translated from Latin into Old English by the Anglo-Saxon King Alfred the Great, and into the Middle English of the fourteenth century by Geoffrey Chaucer. Chaucer's version was printed by William Caxton in 1478. In 1593, Boethius's book was translated by Queen Elizabeth I, who was then sixty years old. In the Middle Ages, the popularity and influence of the book were phenomenal.

The *Consolation* centres around a dialogue between the author and a female personification of philosophy itself. It is written in comparatively simple language, lacking Cassiodorus' flourishes. For generations of readers the book provided a link between the pagan philosophers of antiquity – among them Socrates, Plato and Aristotle – and the world-view of the Christians, of whom Boethius was one. Gibbon sums it up in typically grand style:

While Boethius, oppressed with fetters, expected each moment the sentence or the stroke of death, he composed, in the tower of Pavia, the Consolation of Philosophy; a golden volume not unworthy of the leisure of Plato or Tully [meaning Cicero], but which claims incomparable merit from the barbarism of the times and the situation of the author. The celestial guide [Philosophy herself], whom he had so long invoked at Rome and Athens, now condescended to illumine his dungeon, to revive his courage, and to pour into his wounds her salutary balm.

Since Boethius's time, other notable works have been written in prison, including the *Travels* of Marco Polo, Walter Raleigh's *History of the World* and John Bunyan's *Pilgrim's Progress*.

It is natural to ask, what was Boethius's relative Cassiodorus doing while the author of the *Consolation* was being tried, locked up, tortured and killed? All we know is that Cassiodorus did not mention Boethius's grim fate in his *Variae*, though, writing as Theodoric, he did praise the accuser Cyprian in that compilation of letters, recommending Cyprian to the senate as the worthy new occupant of the exalted position of count of the sacred largesses. The son of an admirable father, Cyprian had proved his worth as a servant of the state, particularly in the courts of law. As a legal adviser, Cyprian had ridden with Theodoric while filling him in, in an entertaining way, on the details of important cases. In an embassy to the East (during which he may have caught wind of a possible plot against the Ostrogoth king) he had conducted himself admirably.

Cyprian's promotion may have happened in the same year Boethius was killed in his prison at Pavia. Around the same time, Cassiodorus rose to the position of *magister officiorum*, a post which had previously been held by the author of the *Consolation*. Can it be that since both men benefited from the fall of Boethius, we can assume that both plotted against him? This would certainly explain why Cassiodorus kept the death of Boethius out of his *Variae*, compiled after his relative's death, and why he included so many words in praise for Boethius's accuser.

It may be that Cyprian accused Boethius not out of sly self-interest but because he thought the philosopher really was a threat to Theodoric, and believed, as Cassiodorus seemed to believe, that Italy was better-off with the Gothic king than with some future replacement supplied by the emperor of the East. In any case, the Gothic king's murder spree did not end with Boethius. Shortly after the death of the philosopher, his father-in-law Symmachus was also executed on Theodoric's orders. This time the deed was done in Ravenna itself. It may be that he had openly opposed the death of his son-in-law, and that that had aroused the king's suspicions.

Just like his son-in-law, Symmachus, who seems to have been a very dignified, capable and honourable man, features in Cassiodorus' *Variae*. Cassiodorus, writing as Theodoric, writes to Symmachus in terms of great respect, spurring him on to sort out tricky legal cases. The king also commends Symmachus for the excellent work he had done, building and re-building in Rome and her suburbs.

The historian Procopius, a younger contemporary of Cassiodorus, who wrote in Greek and was very much a child of the eastern empire, supplies a bizarre account of the death of Theodoric, which happened in August 526. Guilt-stricken over the murder of Symmachus, whom Gibbon calls 'an innocent and aged senator', the Gothic king started to behave very oddly when a fish, complete with its head, was served up as his dinner. In the words of Dewing's translation of Procopius's *Gothic War*, the fish's head:

. . . seemed to Theodoric to be the head of Symmachus newly slain. Indeed, with its teeth set in its lower lip and its eyes looking at him with a grim and insane stare, it did resemble exceedingly a person threatening him. And becoming greatly frightened at the extraordinary prodigy and shivering excessively, he retired running to his own chamber, and bidding them place many covers upon him, remained quiet. But afterwards he disclosed to his physician Elpidius all that had happened and wept for the wrong he had done Symmachus and Boethius. Then, having lamented and grieved exceedingly over the unfortunate occurrence, he died not long afterward.

The Ostrogoth king of Italy was laid to rest, probably in a re-purposed deep-red porphyry bath-tub, inside the grand mausoleum he had built for himself outside Ravenna. The building is plain, heavy-looking and grimly impressive. The top half suggests the armoured head of some warlike monster in a science-fiction film, and is capped by a dome-shaped cover comprising a single piece of stone weighing some two hundred and thirty metric tons. As a source called the *Anonymus Valesianus* states, Theodoric's tomb was 'a work of extraordinary size, and [he] sought out a huge rock to place upon it' (from the Loeb edition, 1939).

Theodoric did not lie long here, and the exact whereabouts of his remains is now unknown. When the forces of the eastern empire pushed the Goths off the throne of Italy, Theodoric's unique mausoleum was converted into a chapel.

After Theodoric

Due to a lack of suitable surviving sons and sons-in-law, after Theodoric's death his throne was occupied by an eight year-old child, his grandson Athalaric. The boy-king was the son of Theodoric's daughter Amalasuentha and her husband Eutharic, perhaps a slightly older contemporary of Cassiodorus and a prince of the Ostrogoths from what we now call Spain. He is remembered in Cassiodorus' *Chronica* as a particularly popular and effective consul, in the year 519. One of the duties of a consul was to put on games, and Eutharic's games staged in Rome were evidently something special. In the words of Bouke Procee's 2014 translation:

He exhibited wild beasts of various kinds in the amphitheatres, at which the present age marvelled for their novelty. And for his spectacles, Africa in its devotion sent over the choicest of delights as well.

When Eutharic 'returned to the sight of his glorious father at Ravenna' (really his father in-law) he staged equally spectacular games there. Unfortunately the promising Eutharic died in 522, at the age of forty-two.

The possibility that a small child might become a king is of course one of the disadvantages of the monarchical system, especially in those days when young princes like Eutharic, the fathers of small children, were likely to die violent premature deaths. The ascendancy of an infant was something that happened repeatedly in the history of the Scottish kings, and Shakespeare depicts some of the problems of such a situation in his history plays.

Both Richard II and Henry VI of England were crowned as children, and in their respective plays the man from Stratford shows them trying to pull themselves out from under the power of the protectors chosen to guide them into adulthood. At the beginning of his play, Richard banishes the son of his protector, the rich and powerful John of Gaunt, thus destabilising the politics of the whole country. Throughout his three plays (*Henry VI* parts I, 2 and 3) the son of the warlike Henry V seems too pious and trusting to rule a country.

In the case of little Athalaric, his mother, Theodoric's daughter Amalasuintha, acted as regent, and was aided (not just as a writer of letters) by Cassiodorus, who as we know had become *magister officiorum* around the time Boethius and Symmachus were killed. By this time Cassiodorus would have been around forty years old. Among letters written by Cassiodorus for the child-king, and included in his *Variae*, are triumphal proclamations of the accession of the new monarch, and, as we have seen, the letter in which

Cassiodorus extols the excellent qualities of both himself and the earlier generations of his family.

The letters including the sad news of Theodoric's death, and the happy news of his grandson's accession, had to be sent to various people and groups. These included the emperor Justin, the Roman Senate, the Roman people, and all the Goths who had settled in Italy. 'Athalaric' told the last group that all the Goths in Ravenna had sworn allegiance to him, and that they, the remaining Italian Goths, should do likewise.

The Emperor Justin, who is supposed to have signed his naming using a stencil, just like Theodoric, must have had Athalaric's letter read aloud to him. In it, Cassiodorus wrote on Athalaric's behalf that the new king of the Ostrogoths sought the emperor's friendship: 'on this friendship,' he wrote, 'I have an hereditary claim. My father [Eutharic] was adorned by you with the palm-enwoven robe of the consul and adopted as a son in arms, a name which I, as one of a younger generation, could more fittingly receive'.

By this time what Justin made of Cassiodorus' letter may not have mattered. Already well over seventy, to judge from the historian Procopius he was losing his faculties and becoming a laughing-stock. For some time the real power had lain with his nephew Justinian, who would become emperor himself when his uncle Justin died in 527.

To judge by the *Variae*, under Athalaric life in Italy and the other parts of Europe that had been controlled by Theodoric continued to plod along much as it had under Athalaric's celebrated grandfather. Cassiodorus' letters written in the young king's name emphasise how much

Athalaric resembles his grandfather, how Theodoric had chosen him as his successor, and how sadness at the news of the death of Theodoric should be tempered with joy that his splendid dynasty was continuing.

The royal letters still commend appointees Athalaric has supposedly chosen for the senate and other honours, the new king still dabbles in the politics of the papacy, and cajoles and threatens wrong-doers. The ghost-writer Athalaric inherited continues to test the patience of his readers by including irrelevant and tangential material, such as an account, in a letter informing one Arator of his promotion, of the invention of writing by the god Mercury:

... I may mention that, according to some, letters were first invented by Mercury, who watched the flight of cranes by the Strymon [the River Struma, that flows through Bulgaria and Greece] and turned the shapes assumed by their flying squadron into forms expressive of the various sounds of the human voice.

Despite his tortuous style, Amalasuintha, who in effect ruled through her little son, had good reason to trust Cassiodorus, as her father had done. By this time our author was evidently counted as a loyal member of the unofficial pro-Gothic party in Ravenna, and had served Theodoric for nearly thirty years. While trying to construct a coherent chronology for Cassiodorus' life, O'Donnell points out that he must have spent time away from Theodoric's side, somewhere other than Ravenna or wherever the royal court happened to be. In this respect, Cassiodorus resembled many well-known figures in British history, who withdrew from official duties at the highest level, sometimes for years at a time, because new favourites had emerged to replace them, or because they had displeased the reigning monarch.

For the Romans, the classic case of the leader who ducks in and out of office was Cincinnatus, a statesman of the fifth century BCE who famously retired from office to 'take up his plough'. He returned only when needed by the state to secure a military victory, then retired back into obscurity. The U.S. city of Cincinnati is named after him.

In this connection, it is useful to remember the sixteenth-century French philosopher Michel de Montaigne, who even turned down earnest invitations from the King of France to become part of his court, because he preferred the company of his books, on his country estate at Guyenne. Like Montaigne, Cassiodorus may have returned to his estates, in his case in Calabria, as his grandfather had done, refusing official honours after his triumphant embassy to Attila.

Whatever Cassiodorus was doing during his absences from court life, it is likely that he spent some of his time there writing. It may have been around 519, when he was perhaps in his mid-thirties, that he wrote or began his monumental *History of the Goths* in twelve volumes. In his letter written during the reign of Athalaric, in which he was obliged to shine a light on his own achievements, Cassiodorus wrote:

Not satisfied with extolling living Kings, from whom he might hope for a reward, he drew forth the Kings of the Goths from the dust of ages, showing that the Amal family had been royal for seventeen generations, and proved that the origin of the Gothic people belonged to Roman history, adorning the whole subject with the flowers of his learning gathered from wide fields of literature.

Unfortunately this work is now lost, but a version of it survives in the form of the *Getica* of Jordanes, himself a Goth, who tells us in his preface that his little book, which takes up fewer than a hundred pages in English translation, is a summary of Cassiodorus' *History*, written at the request of one Castalius, evidently a reluctant or lazy reader. Also in his preface, Jordanes admits that he did not have a copy of Cassiodorus' original to hand when he wrote his *Getica*, though he had read it through at some point in the past and had asked the author himself to lend him a copy. Jordanes seems not to have had the privilege of even a brief meeting with Cassiodorus at this time; the author's steward only allowed him to keep a copy for three days, so that, as Jordanes says, 'The words I recall not, but the sense and the deeds related I think I retain entire' (from Charles C. Mierow's translation).

In the introduction to an edition of his translation, Mierow tries to identify Jordanes and trace possible connections to his contemporary, Cassiodorus. He suggests that the author of the stripped-down Gothic history was one Bishop Jordanes of Crotone, a seaside place in Calabria, the region of Italy where, as we know, Cassiodorus' family owned land. Can it be that Jordanes had begged a manuscript of the original *Gothic History* from the author, his neighbour, when they were both in that part of the world?

In those days, this would not have been as easy as it would be today. Squillace, near which the estates of the

Cassiodori were located, is some fifty miles south-west along the Italian coast from Cortone – at best a return trip of four days on horseback. Given how long it would have taken to do it that way, it seems odd that Cassiodorus, or his steward, only allowed the poor bishop (if such he was) to keep the manuscript three days. Perhaps Jordanes decamped to somewhere nearer Squillace, or maybe both men where in Ravenna when Jordanes felt the need to refresh his memory of what Cassiodorus had written about the Goths. It is also possible that Jordanes enjoyed his second, brief exposure to Cassiodorus' Gothic history when both men were living in Constantinople.

Either way, Cassiodorus might have wanted Jordanes to have limited access to his book, since he knew that Jordanes was a poor writer, with an uncertain grasp of correct Latin grammar and spelling. Mierow calls his Latin 'uncouth and barbarous', and points out, with a shiver, that the author's poor spelling meant that for him 'the accusative is often identical in form with the ablative'. As if that were not bad enough, fourth declension words 'are now changed to the second', and 'third declension adjectives changed to the second declension'. As well as screwing up his face at Jordanes' Latin (if he was ever unfortunate enough to come across an example) Cassiodorus may also have been reluctant to help too much in the production of a new history of the Goths (re-using his own hard-won material) that might compete with his own.

Schoolboy errors in writing style are not the only flaws in Jordanes' *Getica*. In an attempt to find links between the ancient history of the Goths and the legends of Greece and

Rome, the author claims that those famous female warriors, the Amazons, were actually Goths, and that the Goths of long ago fought wars against the ancient Egyptians. Jordanes also confuses various nations – the title *Getica* makes this evident, as the Getae were not Goths. Another reason why Cassiodorus may not have wanted Jordanes to have much exposure to his own *Gothic History* may be because he intended that work to establish the Goths in the minds of his readers as an ancient, wise and warlike race. He may have feared that a version by Jordanes, riddled with mistakes, would expose the Goths to ridicule.

Ridiculous as it may seem, the habit of fabricating an ancient history for a nation who are newly-arrived on the world stage has been fairly common throughout history. The Romans themselves asserted that they were descended from Aeneas, a prince of the Trojans, who was a noble refugee from the ruined city of Troy. Their national epic was therefore the *Aeneid* of Virgil. The British also used to claim descent from a Trojan prince, in our case one Brutus, hence the name 'Britain'. The Mormons are also supposed to believe that the Native Americans are descended from a lost tribe of Israel that somehow managed to cross the Atlantic.

Scholars have long argued over what parts of Jordanes' *Getica* come from Cassiodorus and which were added by Jordanes from other sources. As Jordanes was himself a Goth, it is not surprising that what seems to come straight from Cassiodorus is the sympathetic treatment of the Goths as a people and a praiseworthy element in European history. The same impression is conveyed in Cassiodorus' *Chronica*, which as we know is primarily a list of Roman consuls. As the *Chronica* nears his own time, the author interrupts his list several times with positive statements, particularly about the glorious Ostrogoth, Theodoric. In the entry for 514, the year of his own consulship, Cassiodorus cannot resist mentioning that a major dispute that had riven the Church was settled in that year, though what had happened to bring peace and unity was that Pope Symmachus, a focus for widespread discontent, died (this was not the same Symmachus who was killed by Theodoric).

The odd status of the *Getica*, both written by and not written by Cassiodorus, makes it similar to much of the *Variae*, written by Cassiodorus in someone else's name. Though his *Getica* glorifies the achievements of his own race, the rule of the Gothic kings of Italy ended soon after Jordanes completed that work, around 551. It may have ended earlier, near the beginning of Athalaric's reign, if an expected invasion, perhaps by the Vandals from North Africa, had actually materialised. In the letter Cassiodorus wrote in the person of Athalaric praising himself, we see the author in the unlikely role of military commander:

For when the care of our shores occupied our royal meditation, he suddenly emerged from the seclusion of his cabinet, boldly, like his ancestors, assumed the office of General, and triumphed by his character when there was no enemy to overcome. For he maintained the Gothic warriors at his own charges, so that there should be no robbery of the Provincials on the one hand, no too heavy burden on the exchequer on the other. Thus was the soldier what he ought to be, the true defender, not the ravager of his country.

We have no way of knowing how well Cassiodorus would have fared as a general if an invading force of Vandals had indeed materialised on the Italian coast. As it turned out, the author was rather like a man who erects a splendid marquee, just in case it rains on the garden-party, a marquee that is not needed because it is dry in the garden all day. From the account in Cassiodorus's *Variae*, he certainly seems to have mastered the logistical side of things; recruiting an army of Goths, getting them to the right place, and feeding and paying them properly so that they did not need to loot or pillage.

Though Athalaric's mother Amalasuentha was evidently a forceful and intelligent woman, who was fluent in Latin, Gothic and Greek, she was threatened by the influence of her fellow-Goths, who among other things disapproved of the way she was raising little Athalaric. Amalasuentha was a woman of some learning, and she wanted her son to have a similar education. She sent him to school, and picked out as his playmates three wise old men, all of them Goths. This and the regent's mild treatment of her son's Italian subjects enraged one faction among the Goths, who even objected to her 'chastising' her son. They suspected that she planned to kill Athalaric, and a delegation of influential Gothic men demanded that she change the style of the young monarch's education out of all recognition.

To them, book-learning seemed effeminate, and the constant company of old men likely to cause Athalaric to grow up weak and cowardly. They also reminded the regent that her father Theodoric had been against the use of teachers, since they caused their students to fear corporal punishment. How could such boys learn *not* to fear swords and spears in later life? Amalasuentha's unwelcome advisers recommended that Athalaric's teachers be cashiered, and the boy given companions of his own age.

The young king ended up with new friends who were a little older than he was, and they quickly introduced him to drink and girls. He was soon so utterly depraved that he paid no attention to his mother, and left her to try to cope alone with the rising dissatisfaction that was becoming evident among their own people. Although it had been a delegation of Goths who were against learning that had forced the queen to change her approach to her son's upbringing, it was a well-educated Goth who proved to be the greatest threat.

It seems that a life of wine, women and song did not agree with Athalaric's constitution. He wasted away and died at the age of sixteen, leaving his royal mother fearfully vulnerable. For help she turned to her cousin Theodahad, the well-educated Goth who was to be her nemesis.

After Athalaric

Theodahad features in Cassiodorus' *Variae* as the subject and recipient of letters supposedly sent by Theodoric concerning his frankly criminal activities. A slightly older contemporary of Cassiodorus, nephew of Theodoric and cousin of Amalasuentha, Theodahad had made himself into a rich landowner in Tuscany, partly by taking over land and property that were not his to take, and squeezing his tenants for maximum profit.

In one letter, 'Theodoric' writes to his nephew, reminding him that vulgar avarice is the root of all evil, and that as a member of the royal family he should not embrace this vice at all. 'The Spectabilis Domitius,' the king continues, 'complains to us that such and such portions of his property have been seized by you with the strong hand, without any pretence of establishing a legal claim to them'. Theodoric warns that he is sending one of his agents to oversee the return of Domitius's stuff. Winding up his letter, Uncle Theodoric reminds his nephew of the importance of *civilitas*, a key word for Cassiodorus that is used throughout the *Variae*.

Later in the *Variae*, we gather that Theodahad is up to his old tricks again, ordering his servants to raid the property of 'the heirs of the Illustrious Argolicus'. After Theodoric's death, his daughter Amalasuentha also felt obliged to curb her cousin's depredations, listening to his victims, and bringing everything to a head at some sort of hearing where, in the words of Procopius, 'being confronted by his denouncers, he had been proved guilty without any question, she compelled him to pay back everything which he had wrongfully seized and then dismissed him'. The man she had humiliated in this way was now the one Amalasuentha called on to help her rule the kingdom of her late son.

In 534 Cassiodorus was called upon to write a letter from Amalasuentha to Justinian, who had now been emperor in the East for seven years. It read in part:

We have promoted to the sceptre a man allied to us by a fraternal tie, that he may wear the purple robes of his ancestors, and may cheer our own soul by his prudent counsels.

Soon Cassiodorus, perhaps with gritted teeth, was writing Theodohad's own letter to the emperor, confirming his new position, and the queen's letter to the Roman senate, in which she called her new co-monarch her brother and 'the fortunate partner of our throne':

Therefore exult, Conscript Fathers, and commend our deed to the blessing of the Almighty. Our sharing our power with another is a pledge of its being wisely and gently exercised. By God's help we have opened our palace to a man of our own race, conspicuous by his illustrious position, who, born of the Amal stock, has a kingly dignity in all his actions, being patient in adversity, moderate in prosperity, and, most difficult of all kinds of government, long used to the government of himself. Moreover, he possesses that desirable quality, literary erudition, lending a grace to a nature originally praiseworthy. It is in books that the sage counsellor finds deeper wisdom, in books that the warrior learns how he may be strengthened by the courage of the soul, in books that the Sovereign discovers how he may weld nations together under his equal rule. In short, there is no condition in life the credit whereof is not augmented by the glorious knowledge of literature.

Amalasuentha's gamble with Theodahad did not end well for her. As regent for her late son, she had felt obliged to execute a number of people whom she suspected of plotting against her. According to Procopius, Theodahad allied himself with the friends and relatives of the queen's victims, and began to have her friends executed. Soon he had banished her to a strong fortress on the tiny island of Marta in Bolsena, one of the Italian lakes. Here Amalasuentha was murdered, and although Theodahad denied any knowledge of or involvement in her killing, Justinian, the eastern emperor, used this as an excuse to launch a vast military campaign to win back Italy from the Goths.

While Justinian and Belisarius, a brilliant military leader, were setting their plan in motion, Cassiodorus found himself writing letters for Theodahad, the new Gothic king of Italy, and also for his wife Gudelina. In a letter to the Roman senate, perhaps written in the spring or summer of 535, it emerges that the king had invited the whole of that august body to come and join him at Ravenna. In the letter, Theodahad/Cassiodorus chides the conscript fathers for refusing to leave Rome because of 'certain foolish anxieties, from which real evil would grow unless the suspicion which caused them could be laid to rest'. Despite his annoyance, his majesty agrees, however, that the majority of the senators can stay put, as long as he can enjoy 'the attendance of certain individuals from your body, as occasion may require, so that on the one hand Rome may not be denuded of her citizens, and on the other that we may not lack prudent counsellors in our chamber'.

In a letter addressed to the people of Rome, included in the *Variae*, Theodahad again takes exception to the ungrateful suspicions of the Romans, who it seems openly resented the presence of some Gothic troops the king had sent there. 'It is not fitting that the Roman people,' he insists, 'should be fickle, or crafty, or full of seditions'. They should appreciate the efforts of the men 'who in their anxiety for your safety have left their homes and families in order to defend you'.

As the threat of invasion from the East began to take form, Cassiodorus was charged with writing letters from Theodahad to Justinian, pleading for peace. At the same time, Gudelina was writing to the empress, Theodora:

Claim this palm of concord between the two States as your own especial crown, that as the Emperor is renowned for his successful wars, so you may receive the praises of all men for this accomplished peace. Let the bearer of these letters see you often and confidentially. We hope for just, not onerous, conditions of peace, although in truth nothing seems impossible to us if we know that it is asked for by such a glorious person as yourself.

The pope at this time was Agapetus I, whom Theodahad sent to Constantinople to sue for peace and ask Justinian to turn back his troops. The pope's unsuccessful mission seems to have had a direct effect on Cassiodorus. He and Agapetus had been trying to raise money to found some schools of Christian scholarship in Rome, but as Cassiodorus explained in his *Institutiones*, which he may have started writing a decade or so after the pope's embassy to Justinian, the project was doomed because of the war then raging in Italy. If Cassiodorus had been hoping that the pontiff would pick up the threads of the scheme after his return to Italy, he was to be disappointed – Agapetus died in the spring of 536.

Under Theodahad, Cassiodorus found himself writing to himself, as praetorian prefect. In one such letter, he asks himself to organise the return of grain to the starving Ligurians and Venetians, who had grown the grain themselves, then had it removed from them as a form of taxation. In another, he asks himself to fix food prices so that the people generally will not starve 'on account of the present barrenness of the land'.

Despite his efforts to make peace with the East, feed his people and suppress exactly the same kind of graft that he had once practised with such enthusiasm, Theodahad did not last long. Belisarius captured Sicily in 535 and began working his way up through Italy. Though he had sued so long for peace, the king was making no preparations for war, though the dreaded invasion was upon him. Suspecting that he planned to give away the Ostrogothic kingdom to Justinian in return for money and asylum, a number of discontented Goths met near the Italian coastal town of

Terracina and elected, unanimously, a replacement for Theodahad. The lucky man was Witigis, an old soldier who had fought in Theodoric's wars. In keeping with tradition, the new king of the Goths was lifted up on a shield 'amid a fence of circling swords'.

Belisarius: from the Nuremberg Chronicle

Witigis appointed one Opilio to track down Theodahad and capture him, dead or alive. At the time, the old king was thought to be on the road, trying to get back to Ravenna from Rome. Opilio had an old grudge against Theodahad, who had prevented his marriage to a rich, beautiful heiress. When he found the Gothic king of Italy, he threw him down and, as Procopius says, 'slew him like a victim for sacrifice'. Once Witigis was established as the new king, he tried to legitimate his claim to the throne by marrying Mataswintha, the daughter of Amalasuentha and sister of Athalaric. He also employed Cassiodorus to write his letters, of which five are preserved in the *Variae*. One, addressed to Witigis's people the Goths, paints a rousing picture of his *al fresco* coronation:

For know that not in the corner of a presence-chamber, but in wide-spreading plains I have been chosen King; and that not the dainty discourse of flatterers, but the blare of trumpets announced my elevation, that the Gothic people, roused by the sound to a kindling of their inborn valour, might once more gaze upon a Soldier King.

In a letter to Justinian, Witigis/Cassiodorus pleads for peace and complains of the damage done by the emperor's armies, 'not in the Provinces alone but in Rome herself, the Capital of the World'. The letter points out that if Justinian wants to punish Theodahad, he, Witigis, has already punished him. If the emperor wants to honour the memory of Amalasuentha, then surely he must befriend the husband of her daughter, 'who has reached by our means that royal station to which your soldiers might well have striven to exalt her, in order that all the nations might see how faithful you remained to the old friendship'.

'In Rome itself, the Capital of the World', which Belisarius captured in the December of 536, Justinian's greatest general restored the city's defences and prepared for a siege. Although he commanded a relatively small force, during the siege of Rome and elsewhere Belisarius's experience and ingenuity frustrated Witigis's efforts to defeat him. A typical example from the siege of Rome, which continued for just over a year, involves the Goths' attempted use of siege towers.

There was much consternation among the Romans as these came trundling across the landscape, but Belisarius merely laughed. He waited for the towers to come within range of a bow-shot, then felled the officer leading the procession with an arrow of his own. He then ordered the soldiers on duty on the wall to shoot at the oxen that were pulling the towers. These were now rendered completely useless.

Understanding that Belisarius had achieved a great deal of success with a very little invasion force, Justinian was now sending reinforcements, and the tide of the war was turning against the Goths. Witigis fled to the safety of Ravenna with its strong defences, as Odoacer had done and as Theodahad had attempted to do. Neither side relished the prospect of another long siege.

It is impossible to understand (or frankly to believe) what happened next without having first grasped the enormous prestige of Belisarius at this time. He not only won battles: he was seen to behave well as a victor, who generally honoured his promises, and made real efforts to control his troops when they resorted to plunder and rapine. He was also a good negotiator, who could, for instance, persuade whole communities to surrender to him, and save much bloodshed.

Before a new, protracted and blood-soaked siege of Ravenna could begin in earnest, *the Goths offered to make Belisarius the king of Italy*. He accepted, and was able to march into Ravenna at the head of a large force, like an honoured guest and not an invader, in May 540. As Gibbon writes:

The day of the surrender of Ravenna was stipulated by the Gothic ambassadors: a fleet, laden with provisions, sailed as a welcome guest into the deepest recess of the harbour: the gates were opened to the fancied king of Italy; and Belisarius, without meeting an enemy, triumphantly marched through the streets of an impregnable city.

It soon emerged that Belisarius had no intention of becoming king of Italy, at the bidding of the Goths or anyone else, and was still loyal to his emperor back in Constantinople. Realising that they had all been duped, it seems that some of the female Goths in the town began to spit in the faces of their menfolk, accusing them of having betrayed their tall selves to the Italians, who were of much shorter stature.

Soon the old empire had regained control of almost the whole of Italy. The one city that remained under Goth control was Pavia in the far north-west, where Boethius had been so cruelly tortured to death during the last days of Theodoric, some sixteen years earlier.

Given his military prowess and his integrity, the reader will not be at all surprised that Belisarius is among those sometimes given the name 'The Last Roman' or 'Last of the Romans'; along with Cassiodorus, Boethius and the emperor Justinian himself. Like Aetius, that other great general of a previous generation, who had known and worked with Cassiodorus' grandfather, Belisarius's success and the immense kudos it brought him provoked the jealousy and suspicion of the emperor. Since no good deed goes unpunished, the general was summoned back to Constantinople; and he brought with him not only many treasures of the Goths, but also Witigis himself, his aristocratic young wife Mataswintha and many of his followers. Among the treasures of the Goths that Belisarius brought home to Constantinople may have been one Magnus Aurelius Cassiodorus Senator.

Among those Cassiodorus left behind, if it is true that he was obliged to head east at this time, was his friend Dionysius Exiguus ('Denis the Small'), who would have been around seventy years old at this time, and had been living and working in Rome for some forty years. Cassiodorus would later write about the astonishing intelligence of this man, which he combined with a rich palette of scholarly skills and a monkish humility.

It seems that Little Denis could translate from Greek into Latin or Latin to Greek so quickly and accurately that it seemed miraculous. He also seems to have had endless stamina, which allowed him to make important compilations of Church laws that are still used today. Like Cassiodorus himself, he is one of those important people who remain generally unknown. It is Dionysius we have to thank for the invention of the BC-AD system of counting the years, which has only recently been altered to BCE-CE.

Before Dionysius Exiguus, Romans either went by the years certain consuls were in charge, or counted years from the birth of the Roman emperor Diocletian, a notorious persecutor of Christians. The so-called 'Era of the Martyrs' is still used by the Coptic Orthodox Church of Alexandria in Egypt, for whom, for instance, our year 2000 was 1716.

Among the books produced at the monastery Cassiodorus set up on his family's lands in Calabria was a so-called 'computus', probably written by Cassiodorus himself in 562. This is the earliest surviving medieval work that uses the BC/AD system of the author's friend Dionysius Exiguus. The short and simple manual was designed to help the reader calculate the year, and the correct date of Easter, among other things.

Cassiodorus' friend Dionysius Exiguus died in Rome in 544, that is, four years after Belisarius's triumphal entry into Ravenna. It cannot be said that the old scholar lived his last years during a golden age for Italy. Those Italians who had welcomed Belisarius and the other Byzantine generals into Italy because they wanted to see a return to the good old days of direct Roman imperial rule were to be bitterly disappointed.

With the noble Belisarius safely back in the city on the Bosphorus, Justinian could go ahead and do with Italy what he had always planned to do, in the event that it could be re-incorporated into the empire. The avaricious emperor attempted to turn the peninsular into nothing more than a cash-cow: a steady source of income. Instead of the noble Belisarius, the Italians now had to contend with Alexander the logothete, a logothete being the Byzantine equivalent of a government minister.

This particular logothete went by the nick-name of *Psalliction*, meaning 'Snips' or 'Alexander the Scissors' because of his special skill, which was clipping coins. He snipped away at everything else too, and filled his own pockets and those of the emperor with the rich clippings. The soldiers who had helped win back Italy for the empire found their pay cut back to little or nothing, while the hapless tax-payers were forced to shell out so much that they had little left for themselves.

As the pips began to squeak, the people started to long for something like the golden days of Theodoric, whose intentions, at least as represented in the letters written for him by Cassiodorus, often seemed very honourable, and who did not appear to be obsessed with monetary gain at any cost, like Theodahad, and now John the Scissors. A new hero now arose from the last city still held by the Goths. A fresh Gothic king called Ildibad set out from Pavia to impose his authority on Italy, though he only commanded about a thousand soldiers. So great was the confusion and dissatisfaction at the time, though, that many flocked to Ildibad's standard, including a large number of unpaid deserters from the imperial army. After he won a battle at Treviso in the north-east in 541, everything north of the river Po was his, but he was assassinated later that year.

Ildibad was eventually replaced by his nephew Totila, of whom Gibbon wrote that he 'was chaste and temperate; and none were deceived, either friends or enemies, who depended on his faith or his clemency'. He continued with Ildibad's policy of winning discontents to his cause, and in the areas he conquered he made a point of collecting a fair amount of tax, and preventing his growing army from perpetrating any outrages. Although Justinian had now sent Belisarius back to Italy to counter the new threat, Totila took city after city and eventually captured Rome itself on the seventeenth of December 546.

At this time, Belisarius was bed-bound with fever, but when he heard that Totila, who had characteristically put a stop to the wholesale massacre of the Roman citizens, was planning to level the city, he sent a letter to the Gothic conqueror, begging him not to do so. Totila complied, but still threw down a third of Rome's outer walls, so that the city would now be impossible to defend, or so he thought. Belisarius thought differently. When he at last rose from his sick-bed, he visited a deserted Rome with a thousand men, and saw that, with some re-building of the walls, it could be changed back into a fortress city. When Totila tried to re-take it, he was repulsed, and in 549 Belisarius was allowed to return to Constantinople. In the same year, Totila managed to re-take Rome, and Justinian, who had not funded Belisarius's campaign against Totila at all adequately, was finally minded to send a respectable force to Italy. This was to be commanded by one Germanus, his cousin, who had married the Gothic princess Mataswintha after her husband, Witigis the deposed king of Italy, died in exile.

Germanus never reached Italy, but made Mataswintha a widow for a second time by dying after a short illness before he arrived. Justinian replaced him with a most unlikely military commander – a seventy-four year-old Armenian palace eunuch called Narses. An experienced and cunning general, Narses seems to have had unlimited funds behind his expedition, which may have set off, in 551, with as many as thirty thousand men. After a series of sieges and pitched battles the elderly Armenian had effectively broken the power of the Goths in Italy, by around 554. Totila is thought to have died either at or shortly after the Battle of Taginae in the summer of 552, when the superior tactics of Narses, particularly his clever use of archers, eventually routed the army of the Goths.

Fifteenth-century impression of Constantinople

The Valley of the Shadow of Death

In 540 CE, the year after Belisarius had marched into Ravenna and broken the unwelcome news that he did not intend to become king of Italy, an unwelcome guest arrived in Egypt, the like of which had never, as far as we know, been seen in the Mediterranean world before. Modern science has confirmed what medical historians have long suspected; that the unexpected visitor was bubonic plague. The presence of this deadly disease, which did not burn itself out until around 549, meant among other things that the character of the Gothic wars in Italy after 541 was quite different from what Belisarius had known up to 540.

Every aspect of military activity, from recruitment to army pay to deployment in battle and the burial of the dead, was effected by the plague or the threat of the plague, and it is surely no coincidence that the likes of Narses could not finally mop up the remaining Gothic threat in Italy until the pestilence was no longer a factor in the Roman world. Of course the plague would return, most notably as the Black Death of the fourteenth century, which may have killed as many as half of the population of Europe.

The sixth century plague, called Justinian's Plague after the Roman emperor of the time, may have killed a hundred million people; perhaps half the human population of the planet. It was concentrated around the Mediterranean basin, and Constantinople was particularly badly hit: Justinian himself contracted it, but recovered, in 542. Procopius, the historian and one-time aide to Belisarius, was present in Constantinople during the worst months of the visitation, and recorded how on some days more than five thousand people died. This meant that all the old tombs filled up, the grave-diggers were unable to dig fast enough, and the living resorted to stuffing the dead into the towers that stood along the city's defensive walls.

Since workers in every conceivable walk of life were sick or dead, the economy went into a tailspin, and some plague victims who might have pulled through died of starvation. In his *Secret History*, Procopius revealed how Justinian still expected the owners of farms to pay the full amount of their usual taxes, though they had no surviving workers to bring in the harvest. The rapacious emperor even obliged them to pay the taxes of their dead neighbours. Houses and other buildings stood empty, and it became rare to see anyone walking in the streets. Terrified, some wicked people reformed their lives but, Procopius remarks, soon returned to their old ways when the danger was past.

Constantinople's strong natural and artificial defences were no match for the devastation wrought by rats disembarking from the ships that brought Egyptian grain to Justinian's capital. In those days nobody had any idea that the fleas on the rats and other mammals were vectors of the pestilence, though Procopius noted how bubonic plague tended to spread from coastal areas, pushing inexorably inland.

The medics of the time were baffled by the disease, but Procopius reports that some people actually saw the demons that were believed by some to bring the sickness, either in their dreams or when they were wide awake:

Now at first those who met these creatures tried to turn them aside by uttering the holiest of names and exorcising them in other ways as well as each one could, but they accomplished absolutely nothing, for even in the sanctuaries where the most of them fled for refuge they were dying constantly. But later on they were unwilling even to give heed to their friends when they called to them and they shut themselves up in their rooms and pretended that they did not hear, although their doors were being beaten down, fearing, obviously, that he who was calling was one of those demons.

(trans. H.B. Dewing)

It is curious that though Procopius was in Constantinople at this time, where Cassiodorus was at least usually resident, and although Cassiodorus certainly *had been* an important figure in the old Gothic government of Italy, the historian never mentions him in any of his voluminous writings. This may suggest that Cassiodorus really wasn't as important as the sources imply; but there is also the possibility that during his long career as a government servant our author had perfected the art of vanishing into the background during dangerous times. This may be what saved him from Theodoric's purge, when Boethius and Symmachus fell under suspicion. By the time Procopius reached the plague-stricken city on the Bosphorus, the man from Calabria may have assumed his new identity of pious has-been, and the future author of *The Gothic Wars* may not even have been aware of his presence at all.

If the plague had struck the western empire in the days of Theodoric, Cassiodorus might have stayed by the king's side, helping direct relief efforts, writing letters to grain merchants, perhaps, warning them not to charge starvation prices in a time of shortage. Alternatively, the author may have fled back to his native Calabria, in the belief that the disease was less likely to spread to a remote, sparsely-populated region. Although the strategy of escaping to the country worked for the young Florentine story-tellers featured in Boccaccio's *Decameron*, there were also risks associated with sheltering in the countryside, where farm-animals could carry the plague-fleas just as well as rats.

Although we know that Cassiodorus may have been in Constantinople at this dangerous time, we know next to nothing about how he lived there and how much freedom he would have had, as an exiled supporter of the old Gothic kings and queens of Italy, to get out of the city and find safety elsewhere. He is unlikely to have had any real official status or position in Constantinople, although various clues suggest that he had access to some sort of decent income while he was there, perhaps from his Calabrian estates. In the worst plague months, Cassiodorus may simply have become one of the people Procopius mentions, who stayed at home and hoped that their firmly-shut doors would keep out both the infection and the demons that were supposed to bring it.

As a stay-at-home internal refugee from the plaque, Cassiodorus would have been like the millions of people who found themselves locked down during the Covid pandemic that began in 2019. In the UK many of us were paid government furlough money because we could not work, and though some became bored and frustrated, others embarked on ambitious projects they had long longed to have the time and leisure to complete. These included grandiose DIY schemes, the rediscovery of their artistic painting skills and the completion of that stupendous thousand-page novel that was only half-finished when they graduated from college.

Such projects are sometimes taken up by people who have recently retired, and of course in the UK many people took the arrival of the Covid virus as a cue to finish work for good and live on their pensions. When Cassiodorus arrived in Constantinople, either in the entourage of king Witigis or independently, he would have been around sixty, an age at which many modern people in the West would like to retire, even though they can reasonably expect to live for another twenty years or so. Sixty was old by the standards of the sixth century, and as plague-ridden Constantinople rapidly became the valley of the shadow of death mentioned in Psalm twenty-three, our author may have looked to the health of his soul; as well as regularly, anxiously checking the state of his body, looking for signs of the plague.

It may have been at this time that Cassiodorus began or continued to write his lengthy and detailed commentary on the Psalms, the *Expositio Psalmorum*. He had already dipped his toe in the vast pool of theological writing with his little treatise on the soul, *De anima*. This employed a systematic approach similar to that still used by some types of modern commentators on scripture. *De anima* tackles such tricky questions as the reason the soul is called *anima*, what its nature and virtues are, and where it might be located in the body.

Cassiodorus' *Expositio Psalmorum* became one of the ancestors of the endless books that have been published and re-published over the years, in which authors have picked through parts of the Bible (or sometimes the whole Bible) verse by verse, offering insights and ideas about the meaning and significance of the texts, their authorship, history, purpose, and many other matters.

In a hefty one-volume commentary on the Psalms that was published in 2003, John Eaton pays attention to ancient and medieval commentators on the Psalms, including Cassiodorus. Eaton also reminds us of the centrality of the Psalms for many medieval Christians. A comprehensive knowledge of these ancient songs of the Jewish people was considered essential, and they were endlessly sung and recited, especially in monastic settings.

It is likely that some monks, mumbling through the psalter half-asleep in a cold dark church at some ungodly hour of the morning, did not quite appreciate the beauty of the Psalms. Not so Cassiodorus, who wrote about how the sacred songs could bring comfort and even joy. Watching the homeless poor of Constantinople dying of plague and starvation in the shelter of the city's endless colonnades, Cassiodorus, the great explainer of the Psalms, may well have thought of Psalm twenty-three, with its assertion that with God as one's shepherd time spent in 'the valley of the shadow of death' need not be fearful. Here is the whole psalm in the King James Version:

1 The Lord is my shepherd; I shall not want.

2 He maketh me to lie down in green pastures: he leadeth me beside the still waters.

3 He restoreth my soul: he leadeth me in the paths of righteousness for his name's sake.

4 Yea, though I walk through the valley of the shadow of death, I will fear no evil: for thou art with me; thy rod and thy staff they comfort me.

5 Thou preparest a table before me in the presence of mine enemies: thou anointest my head with oil; my cup runneth over.

6 Surely goodness and mercy shall follow me all the days of my life: and I will dwell in the house of the Lord for ever.

The psalm is traditionally assigned to King David. Though St Augustine, whose writings Cassiodorus used to illuminate his own thoughts on the Psalms, did not believe that all of them had been composed by King David, apparently Cassiodorus did. One might think, therefore, that the author of the *Expositio Psalmorum* would simply have taken this short psalm for what it appears to be. Surely it is David's expression of his feeling that in the presence of his enemies, with the ever-present threat of danger and despair, the Lord provides for him, bringing him rest, stillness, sustenance, comfort and a sense of home.

Cassiodorus' commentary seems quite the opposite of any straightforward one. For him, the speaker of the poem is an archetypal sinful man who has been led by God to the salvation of baptism: the 'still waters' are the waters of the font, and the table laid out for him is a Christian altar complete with all the paraphernalia of the Mass. Cassiodorus counts ten benefits the Lord bestows on the speaker of the poem, and asserts that these reflect in some mystical way the ten commandments handed down to Moses. Because in the Latin version of the Psalms that Cassiodorus used, this psalm was number twenty-two, not twenty-three, the commentator was able to find an equivalent in the twenty-two books of the Old Testament, as counted by the Jews.

This Christianisation of a characteristically Jewish text introduces odd new elements into the mental picture evoked by the psalm. Instead of young David the shepherd wandering in the wilderness, but finding rest and refreshment there, we find that the wilderness now features a Christian altar, complete with altar cloth and a communion cup or chalice. And somewhere in the picture is a baptismal font.

This approach may seem bizarre, but it was all part of the medieval attempt to turn Judaism, one of the foundations of Christianity, into the kind of foundation that remains firmly underground. Indeed Eaton offers Cassiodorus' treatment of psalm twenty-three as an example of the typical type of medieval interpretation 'as centred in Christ'. This approach remained typical partly because copies of Cassiodorus' influential commentary, which Eaton calls 'serviceable', were to be found in the libraries of many monasteries and other places where the Psalms might be studied, throughout the middle ages and beyond.

Whatever Cassiodorus' status was in Constantinople at this time, it is likely that as a man who had worked at the top of the Italian hierarchy for years during the reigns of the Gothic kings, he would have been subject to some sort of surveillance. One can imagine whoever was in charge of gathering intelligence on the retired government official reporting to his controller within Justinian's secret service, perhaps once a week at first, but being unable to report anything more than that the man was still working on his Psalms commentary. Eventually these meetings would be re-scheduled for once a fortnight, then once a month, then perhaps they were discontinued altogether.

In his treatise on the soul Cassiodorus referred to a range of old pagan authors, as well as Christian ones, to support his findings. The range of references in his *Expositio Psalmorum* reflects well on the availability of useful supporting texts in sixth-century Constantinople, with its sophisticated literary culture and sumptuous libraries. While both of these works demonstrate how the mind of Cassiodorus could straddle different worlds – the Jewish, the ancient classical and the Christian medieval worlds, the city on the Bosphorus, where he may have lived for as many as fifteen years or more, managed to contain these worlds and more in its dizzyingly diverse self.

There were probably Jews living in Constantinople even before it became Constantinople, and it is interesting to imagine how they responded to the rich visual culture of the Byzantine Christians. Not only were there glittering mosaics depicting various episodes and characters from scripture; there were also works in two and three dimensions that seemed to elevate present and past emperors to the status of gods. There were pagan statues and temples, and some of the statues of the old gods were even placed inside the churches. The residual paganism of the superstitious citizens meant that many believed that these idols still had power. It was long believed, for instance, that if an unfaithful wife or a counterfeit virgin touched a certain statue of Venus, she would not be able to stop herself tearing off all her clothes.

The statue of Venus that was supposed to have this power was part of the external decoration of a brothel, but there were many much more sober and spiritual places in Constantinople. These included monasteries and their libraries, and one can imagine Cassiodorus, his steward or one of his other servants befriending all sorts of learned and pious people who might be able to help with ideas and sources.

The sense of Constantinople at this time as both an ancient Roman city and a medieval one was also reflected in the nature of the entertainments laid on for the people. The cruel gladiatorial combats of old were now off the menu – they were inconsistent with Christian ideas of love and mercy – but plenty of carnage could still be seen during the chariot-races, and the street-fights between fans of the rival teams of charioteers.

A more cerebral type of enjoyment could be extracted from the theological disputes that came in waves over the city, like plagues, storms or earthquakes. We owe our best piece of independent evidence of Cassiodorus' presence in Constantinople at this time to just such a disagreement. The controversy centred around certain writings of three fifth-century theologians; Theodore of Mopsuestia, Theodoret of Cyrus and Ibas of Edessa. These became known as the Three Chapters, and the emperor Justinian, who believed that he should have power over the Church (and even over the religious practices of the Jews) condemned them.

At first Vigilius, the Pope at the time, refused to anathematise the Three Chapters, but eventually brought himself in line with the emperor. In keeping with his new negative attitude to the offending texts, Vigilius wrote a letter in 550, excommunicating two men, Rusticus and Sebastianus, who disagreed. Cassiodorus was mentioned in the letter, and called by the pope a *religiosus vir*, a man of religion. This, and the work that Cassiodorus probably did at this time in Constantinople on his Psalm commentary, suggests that after years serving a succession of Gothic kings and queens, Cassiodorus was looking for ways to serve the King of Kings.

When he wrote his letter mentioning Cassiodorus, Pope Vigilius himself was in Constantinople, having been, in effect, kidnapped in Rome by imperial agents and forced to go there in the winter of 545. He stayed in Justinian's city for eight years, wrangling over the theological controversy surrounding the Three Chapters, until he finally agreed to condemn them. It is possible that he knew Cassiodorus because a clique of Latin-speaking Italian ex-pats had formed around the captive pontiff, and that Cassiodorus was a member of the clique.

The intellectual history of Christianity at this time is littered with theological controversies, which tended to throw up accusations of heresy on both sides. The Three

Chapters controversy was complicated by the fact that the eastern emperor and his wife the empress Theodora felt that it was their place to intervene, and that the contrast between the different beliefs and religious languages of East and West was involved. Indeed Vigilius may have been puzzled because he was unable to read some of the relevant documents for himself, since they were in Greek. A further dimension of complexity was added to the dispute because whereas the supporters of the Three Chapters tended to be Christians from Syria and Egypt, those who were against them, like Justinian, were centred on Constantinople.

The accusation was that the tendency of the Three Chapters was towards Nestorianism, a theological viewpoint promoted by one Archbishop Nestorius of Constantinople, himself a Syrian, who died in the middle of the fifth century. The opinions that had seen Nestorius ejected from his role as archbishop in 431 concerned the nature of Jesus himself, whom Nestorius saw as having two natures: he was both God and a man. The view that prevailed among Roman Catholics after the council of Ephesus in 431 was that Jesus's two natures were inseparable.

Vivarium

After the definitive collapse of Gothic rule in Italy, Cassiodorus' homeland gradually became a more inviting prospect for ex-pat Italians who had been weathering the long military and political storm in Constantinople and elsewhere. The so-called Pragmatic Sanction issued by Justinian in 554 formalised Italy's status as a province of the Byzantine empire. This it seems persuaded many in the Italian diaspora to return home.

Now nearing seventy, Cassiodorus might have been expected to return home to his estates and spend the rest of his life doing the sixth-century equivalent of smoking a pipe in his rocking-chair on the back porch. Not a bit of it. When Cassiodorus returned to Calabria, he either set up, or returned to, a monastery, or rather two monasteries, made to his specifications on his own land. The place acquired the name Vivarium, from the salt-water pools full of fish that supplied the monks with some of their protein. The fish were persuaded to come in from the sea and became trapped in the pools, but in his *Institutiones*, of which more later, Cassiodorus insists that they did not realise that they were trapped, and believed themselves to be inside a sea-cave of some kind.

A supply of fish was important to monastic communities, as meat from mammals and birds could not be eaten on certain days, according to Christian tradition. Today in English a 'vivarium' does not mean something that contains fish at all: the word is usually used for tanks containing smallish creatures that need a particular climate, simulated inside the tank, to survive. Modern vivaria often contain insects, spiders, reptiles or amphibians.

The exact site of Vivarium was determined in the 1930s by the French scholar Pierre Courcelle. Courcelle compared Cassiodorus' own descriptions of the place, in his *Institutiones*, to illustrations found in copies of the *Institutiones* dating from after Cassiodorus' time, but probably based on pictures in manuscripts produced at Vivarium itself. One of these illustrations, from an eighth-century manuscript kept at the state library in the Bavarian town of Bamberg, has all the colourful naivete of the Bayeux tapestry. It shows the monastery church of St Martin in vivid orange and green, with smiling fish swimming into what looks like a small swimming-pool with attractive tiles around the edge. The doomed fish seem too happy to kill a Gothic king by shooting him an accusing glare, even after they had been killed and cooked.

Using his combination of written and painted evidence Courcelle placed Vivarium in what is now the small seaside resort of Copanello de Staletti, at the southern end of the instep of Italy, on the Ionian Sea. Here the pools the monks used to trap their fish can still be seen at the *Scogliera delle*

Vasche di Cassiodoro (Cliffs of the Tanks of Cassiodorus). At low tide, fish are still trapped in these, after nearly fifteen hundred years. From above, the pools or tanks look like the classic Roman or Byzantine type of spoon, with a very long, thin handle or stalk. The handle part is the narrow channel the fish swim up, only to become trapped.

If Cassiodorus devised or improved on this system, it is further evidence of his interest in the natural world, and in human technology. As well as water-clocks and perhaps the astonishing Antikythera mechanism, he also applied his subtle mind to the issue of supplying fish to hungry monks. Other technology used at Vivarium included sundials, water-clocks and, as Hodgkin puts it, 'mechanical lamps of some wonderful construction, which appears to have made them self-trimming, and to have ensured their having always a sufficient supply of oil'.

The pools or tanks at the *Scogliera delle Vasche di Cassiodoro* are overlooked by the scant ruins of the church of St Martin, the twelfth-century replacement for Vivarium's monastery church. The probable dimensions of the church suggest that Vivarium may not have been able to accommodate more than a hundred monks; perhaps far fewer. Nearby in 1952 workmen found a stone coffin that could well be the tomb of the illustrious and long-lived founder of Vivarium.

Cassiodorus' foundation comprised a monastery for monks wishing to live in a community, and another, called Castellum, for brothers who wished to live as hermits. While the gregarious monks lived on the coast, the shyer brothers dwelt a little more inland and half a mile to the north, in the abandoned Greek settlement of Skylletion, now the Scolacium Archaeological Park at Roccelletta. The Roman town of Minervia Scolacium, founded on the site of the Greek Skylletion, is supposed to have been the birthplace of Cassiodorus himself. The modern archaeological park boasts ruined architecture from the Roman, Byzantine and Norman periods, as well as a museum of antiquities; all surrounded by hundreds of olive trees, some over two hundred years old.

It is unclear whether Cassiodorus had started to set up a monastery on his own land long before his return to Italy after his sojourn in Constantinople, or whether he began it from scratch once Justinian's Pragmatic Sanction had brought in a brief period of peace and security. It was certainly not uncommon for wealthy people in the Middle Ages to set up religious communities on land they owned, or land they had given to the Church for that purpose. Some of these donors retired to the monasteries they had founded, endowed or funded, as Cassiodorus did, though for him 'retirement' did not mean an end to work.

Here again we can usefully compare Cassiodorus' life-choices with those of the French Renaissance figure Michel de Montaigne. Having intended to retire and live out the rest of his life in his tower-library, the philosopher found that after a few years he was still fit and clear-headed, and so he set off on his travels. Likewise Cassiodorus, who might have expected to die in his sixties, slumped over the manuscript of his commentary on the Psalms in some rented house in Constantinople, found that he still had energy and a good brain in his seventies, and returned to Calabria with his plans for Vivarium.

An example of a founder of an abbey who retired to it in later life was Queen Balthild, the Anglo-Saxon wife of the French king Clovis II, a lady who was born some forty years after Cassiodorus died. She may have founded as many as five abbeys, and after some years as a widow she retired to one of them, at Chelles near Paris. The arrival of such a distinguished guest, who was in the habit of choosing the abbesses for her monastery, must have been awkward, at times, for the then abbess, who could hardly regard the new member of the community as just another visitor. Medieval royals and other aristocrats who dabbled in religious institutions in this way could impose the secular hierarchy of the feudal world onto them. They could also exert a great deal of influence through abbots, abbesses and bishops whom they had helped into their positions; and often expected their own friends or relatives to be made bishops, abbots or abbesses in turn.

Perhaps the most famous example of an aristocrat founding a monastery is that of St Gregory, otherwise known as Gregory the Great, who was born in Rome when Cassiodorus was around forty-five years old. Unlike Balthild and Cassiodorus, who retired to monasteries they founded, the monastery Gregory set up in the heart of the Eternal City functioned as a springboard that launched the future saint into the role of pope; though he is supposed to have been very reluctant to occupy St Peter's chair.

Buildings that had once housed members of Gregory's distinguished family and their staff were converted into monastic spaces. If Cassiodorus practised a similar type of holy refurbishment down in Calabria, the physical structures that made up Vivarium may have become useful to the monks fairly quickly. In both cases, it is likely that the final set of buildings was arrived at by a combination of adaptation, demolition and new building.

When he arrived at Vivarium some time in the 550s, or when he got to the site that would become Vivarium, Cassiodorus may have been too old to think about exerting undue political influence through his foundation. He had, after all, enjoyed a long and distinguished career, and he may have been all too aware of the dangers of jostling for power with one's ambitious contemporaries, who might turn out to be vicious and vengeful. If Cassiodorus planned to place a nephew or son of his own in a prestigious position in the hierarchy of his new monastery, there is no record of it. In fact there is no hint anywhere that Cassiodorus was ever married, or fathered children.

The easy pipe/rocking-chair/porch retirement plan may have been more attractive to Cassiodorus if he had had a wife, children and grandchildren to share it with. Surely at least one child, or perhaps a son or daughter-in-law, would have opted to stay with Mum and Dad in the old place by the Ionian Sea. As it turned out, Cassiodorus retired not with children or grand-children but with a small band of brothers. One or more of the brethren may have been trusted with the whole business of running the old Calabrian estates of the *Cassiodori*, setting rents, facilitating the collection of taxes, and probably employing lay workers to toil in any farms, orchards, vineyards, mills, forges or factories that belonged directly to the monastery. This was the sort of work that might have been done by a capable son of Cassiodorus, if he had ever had any sons, and if he had not converted his home into a monastery.

It is clear that when Cassiodorus lived there his Vivarium community had a very respectable library, and it may be that during his stay in Constantinople the author had acquired many valuable texts, particularly Greek ones, with the intention of returning with them to Calabria, whether or not his monastery yet existed when he was living in Justinian's city. We know about the library and other aspects of Cassiodorus' foundation, including those mysterious and miraculous lamps, from his book *Institutiones divinarum et saecularium litterarum* (Institutions of Divine and Secular Learning).

As the long version of its title suggests, the book is made up of two halves, dealing with divine and secular literature respectively; but these sections are also carefully sub-divided. The whole book begins with a sort of digest of versions of the Bible, and of the great Christian writers and their works, many of which, like Cassiodorus' book on the Psalms, fall into the category of Biblical commentary. In a charming passage, the author compares Biblical commentaries and their creators to Jacob's ladder, seen in a dream by the Biblical patriarch Jacob, as recorded in chapter twenty-eight of Genesis:

And he dreamed, and behold a ladder set up on the earth, and the top of it reached to heaven: and behold the angels of God ascending and descending on it.

(Genesis 28:12, KJV)

In the same way Jacob's ladder shows a route up to heaven, the best Biblical commentaries, Cassiodorus insists, can give the reader a route into a better understanding of the scriptures, which can then help secure his own entry into heaven after death.

The Biblical commentators Cassiodorus mentions in the first book of his *Institutiones* include some authors who are still famous enough to have been heard of even by people with no interest in the business of Biblical exegesis. These include St Jerome, who gets several references, and St Augustine of Hippo. Both of these learned saints died early in the fifth century, and both are counted as doctors of the church by Roman Catholics. Other Catholic doctors (meaning teachers) mentioned in the *Institutiones* include Ambrose, Gregory the Great and John Chrysostom. Christian scholars who are mentioned, whom Cassiodorus knew personally, include Boethius and Dionysius Exiguus.

Although all the writings of some of the scholars Cassiodorus mentions were considered by the Church to be of unimpeachable fidelity, some, like Origen for instance, were thought to have been guilty of entertaining heretical ideas. Origen, an Egyptian, had died in the middle of the third century, and it may have been not his ideas but those of his later followers that upset the theologians of Cassiodorus' generation. In the same way that Justinian condemned the contents of the controversial Three Chapters, he also anathematised all of Origen's writings, in 543, which may have been shortly after Cassiodorus began his long sojourn in the emperor's city. Justinian even insisted that all of

Origen's works should be burned: if anyone had ever managed to get all the copies of all of them together, this would have made a memorable bonfire: Origen is supposed to have written thousands of theological works.

Despite the fact that he had come under theological suspicion, Cassiodorus still stands up for Origen, to some extent, in his *Institutiones*. He points out that Jerome himself had defended him and translated some of his works into Latin, and suggests, on the authority of some unnamed writer with a poetic turn of mind, that Origen should be treated like aniseed: 'for after he seasons the food of sacred literature, he himself is to be cooked, extracted, and thrown away'. Readers may have had the experience of discovering a whole, cooked, indigestible star anise in a curry: for such readers, Cassiodorus' analogy will seem particularly vivid.

In the first book of his *Institutiones*, Cassiodorus is not writing about his Christian authors in an abstract way, as one might reminisce about books one had borrowed from a library and returned. His comments applied to actual copies of these books held by the library at Vivarium, some of which had been created at the monastery itself. Some of the copying work had been done by Cassiodorus personally, who also, to judge from his *Institutiones*, must have had a lot of influence over what books were copied out, and what new books were to be brought in. Like an obsessive collector striving to, for instance, acquire a copy of every stamp ever printed that bore the image of Queen Elizabeth II, Cassiodorus also mentions books he regards as indispensable, but which the Vivarium library has not yet acquired.

Although Cassiodorus may have been driven by the classic collector's urge to get 'the complete set', he was also very clear that every volume that made it onto his shelves had to play a role in the education of his monks, and the salvation of their souls. Certain passages in Origen might endanger a brother's progress up the Jacob's ladder of Christian understanding, so as a warning Cassiodorus marked these passages with what he calls the achresimon, a warning symbol. Other books at Vivarium had similar markings, and annotations to aid productive reading; and the way some short texts were bound together, and longer texts broken up into volumes, was also calculated to improve their usefulness.

Later at Vivarium, Cassiodorus would go further than merely placing a warning symbol in the margin of passages judged to be heretical. Taking up a commentary on the New Testament letters that had been attributed to Pope Gelasius, who had died when Cassiodorus was still a child, the founder of Vivarium discovered it to be so full of heretical ideas that he started cutting out whole sections. He only got as far as the end of Paul's letter to the Romans, and left the rest to his fellow-monks.

Parts of Cassiodorus' *Institutiones* read like an account of the building of a fine modern library, except that in many cases the Vivarium monks had to make their own books by copying, translating from Greek into Latin, producing redacted versions of longer existing books, or writing something new. To aid in the production of new books, and no doubt to bind or re-bind old ones, the monastery employed skilled binders, as some libraries still do today.

Mentioning his bindery, Cassiodorus writes about another curious bit of technology that, like his remarkable lamps, is hard to visualise. This was a book of samples of different types of bindings. Once a book was finished, its author or copyist could choose how he wanted it to be bound. For binding, the library at Vivarium would have needed a supply of animal skins: they would also have needed skins to make into parchment or vellum for the pages of their books. The parchment could have been bought ready-made, but other medieval monasteries used skins from their own farm animals.

An example of a book created, completed or copied and bound at Vivarium which counted among the library's 'redacted versions of longer existing books' might have been Cassiodorus' *Historia Tripartita*. This is a history of the church running from the year 324 to 439, made up of bits of earlier histories, originally written in Greek but translated into Latin by Epiphanius Scholasticus, one of the monastery's translators whom Cassiodorus names in his *Institutiones*.

The book was undeniably useful, since it picked up from roughly where the earlier Greek church history of the celebrated Eusebius of Caesarea left off. In his *Institutiones*, Cassiodorus suggests that the reader begin with the Jewish historian Josephus (who originally wrote in Greek), go on to the Latin version of Eusebius, then conclude with the *Historia Tripartita*. With a flush of pride, Cassiodorus mentions that Jerome had considered it impossible to put all the massive volumes of Josephus into Latin, but that this had been accomplished by a hard-working team at Vivarium.

The usefulness of books is a real theme in the *Institutiones*, and Cassiodorus does not only mention volumes that might help the religious education and spiritual development of the Vivarium monks. There were also books on medicine (as well as resident medics) and works on agriculture. As well as giving an account of past and current literary activities at Vivarium, Cassiodorus' *Institutiones* hints at future bookish projects, and gives advice on how, for instance, lay workers, and monks with little or no interest in reading, were to be managed, and their souls helped on their way up Jacob's ladder.

Justinian (centre). Belisarius may be the second figure from the left. From a mosaic at Revenna.

Decline and Fall

Throughout the first book of his *Institutiones divinarum et saecularium litterarum*, Cassiodorus reminds us that after his account of the different types of sacred literature, he will be examining secular or profane literature, some of it dating from before Christianity. As in book one, the emphasis here is on usefulness, but still the author feels obliged to justify his attention to these texts, many of which harked back to the paganism that Cassiodorus feared still had a hold on the minds of the local plebeians down in Calabria. These, he urged in his *Institutiones*, must be persuaded to abandon their deplorable habit of worshipping groves once sacred to the pagan gods.

One way the Christian Cassiodorus justifies a grounding in the best of the ancient pagans – Homer, Demosthenes, Cicero, Virgil – is by naming celebrated Christians who had a taste of their culture, including Ambrose, Augustine and Jerome. He also offers the example of Moses, who 'was learned in all the wisdom of the Egyptians', yet still embraced the life and faith of 'his brethren, the children of Israel' (see Acts 7, 22-23).

Book two of Cassiodorus' *Institutiones* is certainly not dedicated entirely to the value for Christians of learning directly about the likes of Homer, Demosthenes, Cicero and Virgil. The book has seven sections, on grammar, arithmetic, rhetoric, dialectic, music, geometry and astronomy; and the author's attempts to summarise the value and content of each of these subjects are frankly a little dry in places. As in the first book of the *Institutiones*, where Cassiodorus seems rather more enthusiastic about his subject-matter, the author regularly name-drops leading figures, and points the reader to the relevant texts available at Vivarium.

The seven categories into which Cassiodorus divided secular knowledge were enormously influential in the middle ages. For centuries, the so-called seven liberal arts were taught to advanced students. These comprised the trivium; grammar, logic and rhetoric, and the quadrivium; arithmetic, geometry, music and astronomy. Cassiodorus was not the first to identify these seven aspects of knowledge, but his *Institutiones* helped to popularise them.

At its end, Cassiodorus' *Institutiones* snaps back from secular knowledge to the Christian world-view. Vivarium's founder suggests that his readers meditate on Revelation, the last book of the Christian Bible, to get a sense what it might be like to really know what is going on in the universe. Cassiodorus also reminds us of Paul's image of the limitations of mere earthly knowledge, however detailed and perfect it tries to be:

For now we see through a glass, darkly; but then face to face: now I know in part; but then shall I know even as also I am known.

(1 Corinthians 13:12)

You can take a horse to water, as they say, but you cannot make it drink. Likewise, you can assemble a group of monks, provide them with good living-conditions and the beginnings of a very useful library; but you cannot make them read, or become profound scholars. In his *Institutiones*, as we have seen, Cassiodorus had addressed the problem of what to do with brothers who were reluctant readers: in two of his last written pieces, the author provided texts for just such monks to read and use. The first is his *Complexiones*, a simple account or explanation of parts of the New Testament.

Also among the last products of Cassiodorus' pen, compiled when he was in his nineties, is his *De orthographia*, a book on spelling that he tells us he was asked to write by his monks. It may be that the fact that such books as *De orthographia* and the *Complexiones* were needed at all at Vivarium, perhaps forty years after their author had arrived there, suggests that Cassiodorus' plan to set up a sort of monastic advanced school of Christian studies on the old family place down in Calabria was an utter failure. After all, the Vivarium library already had books on orthography and the New Testament that a reasonably ambitious reader could consult. Stuffed with happy fish and sumptuously bathed in the facilities the founder had set up, some at least of the monks at Vivarium seem to have become lazy dunces.

O'Donnell couples the possibility of a steep decline in intellectual and literary standards at Vivarium with his attempted demolition of an abiding myth that has hung about Cassiodorus and his Calabrian monastery: that using Vivarium as a kind of intensive care unit for Western European culture, its founder ensured the survival of a mass of ancient Latin and Greek literature, that we can find today in our book-shops and libraries, that would otherwise have been lost. The myth is set out perfectly by Hodgkin, who evidently believed it, in the introduction to his translation of the *Variae*:

The great merit of Cassiodorus . . . was his determination to utilise the vast leisure of the convent for the preservation of Divine and human learning and for its transmission to after ages . . . Cassiodorus resolved to make of his monastery not merely a place for pious meditation, but a theological school and a manufactory for the multiplication of copies, not only of the Scriptures, not only of the Fathers and the commentators on Scripture, but also of the great writers of pagan antiquity.

O'Donnell, writing nearly a century later, found little evidence of this, for instance in the form of surviving copies of the works 'of the great writers of pagan antiquity' that had been produced at Vivarium, or books that were copies from lost 'Vivarian' manuscripts. In fact there may not have been much time for large numbers of such manuscripts to be created at Vivarium, since it is possible that the monastery disbanded shortly after Cassiodorus' death.

Referring to the activities of Benedictine monasteries, governed by the strict monastic Rule written by Benedict himself, Hodgkin asserts that:

. . . using the convent as a place of literary toil and theological training . . . was entirely in harmony with the spirit of the Rule of St. Benedict, if it was not formally ordained in that document. At a very early date in the history of their order, the Benedictines, influenced probably by the example of the monastery of Vivaria, commenced that long series of services to the cause of literature which they have never wholly intermitted.

That 'probably', and Hodgkin's insistence of the importance of something for the Benedictines that was not mentioned in their Rule, look like ingredients in a weak argument, as does his earlier description of 'the vast leisure of the convent'. Some of those monks were busy bees.

Although Vivarium may not have lived up to its reputation as a sort of Noah's ark for ancient secular literature, some of its founder's writings continued to be read, used and revered for hundreds of years after his death. Particularly influential were the commentary on the Psalms (admired by, among others, the Venerable Bede), the treatise on the soul, and the *Institutiones*, though many editions featured only one of its two books. The *Variae*, now the work by Cassiodorus that is most widely available, seems to have been rediscovered late in the medieval period, and is valued today as a source-book for the history of the sixth century.

If readers hoping to find an account of Cassiodorus' single-handed rescue of ancient western culture feel let down at this point, they cannot have been as disappointed as those of Cassiodorus' contemporaries who believed that the fall of the Gothic kings would mean that Italy would now remain both unified, and safely held in the kind but firm embrace of the Roman empire.

When Cassiodorus had been living and working at his Vivarium monastery for more than a decade, and was in his early eighties, the Lombards, another of those restless, land-hungry nations of the Migration Period, began to take over the north of Italy. Both Justinian and Belisarius had died just a few years before the Lombard invasions began: the emperor's successors had no worthy successors of the greatest Byzantine general to throw against the new masters of the north.

The advent of the Lombards in Italy tended to disunite the Italian territory that Justinian had tried to bring together under Byzantine rule, after the last Gothic kings had been defeated. This eventually led to the medieval shape of Italy, made up of separate kingdoms, dukedoms and city-states.

Cassiodorus' native Calabria remained part of the Byzantine empire until the Norman invasion of 1060. Many parts of this region of Italy that had once been colonised by ancient Greeks in the days of Cassiodorus' ancestors now became Greek again, as Byzantine Greeks settled in Calabria. Greek monks who had read about Cassiodorus established monasteries near where Vivarium had been, and Calabria still has a significant minority of Greek-speakers; the Griko people. Their version of Greek, called Griko, can still be heard in nine towns scattered over the extreme southern end of the toe of Italy.

As we have seen, the Roman empire of the East, the Byzantine empire, persisted until Constantinople fell to the Ottoman Turks in 1453. The last Byzantine emperor, Constantine XI Paleologus, died in that historic siege. Some of the citizens who tried to shelter in Justinian's vast cathedral of St Sophia during the Ottoman onslaught may have regarded themselves as the last Romans, though they may not have been able to speak a word of Latin or medieval Italian. They may have been descended from early Roman settlers in Constantinople, but their families could have had Greek names for generations.

Historically-minded fugitives mixing with those who sheltered in St Sophia during the siege, waiting to be raped, killed or enslaved, may have remembered that the title 'last of the Romans' was being banded about even during the time of Julius Caesar. Both Brutus and Cassius, who conspired to assassinate Julius, were regarded as *Ultimas Romanorum*, as was Stilicho, a Roman general from the Vandal nation who died early in the fifth century. We have already seen how Boethius, Belisarius, Justinian, and Romulus Augustulus, the last Roman emperor of the West, as well as Cassiodorus, have been called the last Roman, though none of these feature in the list printed in the latest version of *Brewer's Dictionary of Phrase and Fable*. *Brewer's* does, however, agree that Cassiodorus's grandfather's friend Flavius Aetius might qualify for the distinction.

Though the empire finally collapsed in 1453, *Brewer's* lists a number of last Romans who lived long after that date, including the eighteenth-century English writers Alexander Pope and William Congreve. In such a crowded field, is it possible that Cassiodorus can come first? Certainly he lived at the same time as several other celebrated last Romans, and was born just a few decades after the death of one of the most distinguished candidates, the military leader Flavius Aetius.

That Odoacer actually wrote a letter to Constantinople announcing the surrender of the last Roman emperor of the West surely suggests that the end of an era had just happened. Yes, the empire continued in the East, and the East even recaptured parts of the old western empire, but one reason why Justinian is sometimes counted as the last Roman is supposed to be because he was the last eastern emperor who grew up speaking Latin. Was not the Byzantine empire a Greek empire, that was so different from the old empire of the West that it had less and less to do with that famous backwater, Rome?

If the fall of the West meant the fall of Rome, then it is hardly surprising that so many of Cassiodorus' contemporaries have been called the last Roman. One would expect the last Romans to have been part of that generation, just as one would expect the very last men who had fought in the Great War to have died early in the twenty-first century. But apart from the fact that he outlived all of them, what would put our author ahead of Boethius, Belisarius, Justinian and Romulus Augustulus?

We can perhaps discount Belisarius and Justinian on the grounds that they were more Byzantine than Roman in their outlook. Although Romulus Augustulus was indeed the last western emperor, he had little choice in the matter, and is not known to have achieved much, except his own survival. Boethius, with his extraordinary stoicism, displayed some fine Roman qualities, but his life and his career did not take him in the very varied directions Cassiodorus took.

To have been a high government minister, then a shy scholar, then the founder of a monastery, displays remarkable flexibility, and a comprehensive set of skills. One result is that Cassiodorus as an historical figure is of interest not only to historians of Rome, but also students of the middle ages, enthusiasts for Latin letters, and theologians. In his last role, as the *éminence grise* of Vivarium, Cassiodorus used his knowledge of, among other things, theology, education, librarianship, book-binding, the cultivation of fish, and even lighting design.

This sort of adaptability, shown in the life of Cassiodorus, may be a neglected factor in the survival of Roman civilisation, which though it famously declined and fell, did manage to survive for over two thousand years. Even if, thinking particularly that Cassiodorus had little to do with the characteristic Roman occupation of splitting open human heads, we deny him the title last of the Romans, we might remember Hodgkin's comment, in the introduction to his English *Variae*:

. . . if one were asked to specify any single life which more than another was in contact both with the Ancient World and the Modern, none could be more suitably named than the life of Cassiodorus.

Select Bibliography

Pope Benedict XVI: *Great Christian Thinkers*, SPCK, 2011

Boethius (trans. James, H.R.): *The Consolation of Philosophy*, Elliot Stock, 1897

Cassiodorus (trans Halporn, J.W. and Vessey, M.): *Institutions of Divine and Secular Learning*, Liverpool University Press, 2004

Cassiodorus (trans. Hodgkin, T.): *The Letters of Cassiodorus*, Oxford, 1886

Dunn, Marilyn: *The Emergence of Monasticism*, Blackwell, 2003

Eaton, John: *The Psalms*, T&T Clark, 2003

Herrin, Judith: *Ravenna: Capital of Empire, Crucible of Europe*, Penguin, 2021

Hodgkin, Thomas: *Theodoric the Goth*, Putnam's, 1923

Hughes, Bettany: *Istanbul: A Tale of Three Cities*, W & N, 2017

Jordanes (trans. Mierow, C. C.): *The Origin and Deeds of the Goths*, Princeton, 1908

Lawrence, C.H: *Medieval Monasticism*, Longmans, 2001

Lewis, Jon E.: *Rome: The Autobiography*, Running Press, 2009

Norwich, John Julius: *The Popes*, Chatto & Windus, 2011

O'Donnell, James J.: *Cassiodorus,* University of California Press, 1995

Procopius (trans. Dewing, H.B.): *The Gothic War*, Heinemann, 1919

Procopius (trans. Williamson, G.A. and Sarris, P.): *The Secret History*, Penguin, 2007

Thacker, Alan T.: *Bede and Cassiodorus*, Iona, 2017

For more from the Langley Press, please visit our website at:
www.langleypress.co.uk